# PHILLIPS' BOOK OF GREAT THOUGHTS & FUNNY SAYINGS

A STUPENDOUS COLLECTION
OF QUOTES, QUIPS,
WITTICISMS, PONDERINGS
& HUMOROUS COMMENTS

## BOB PHILLIPS

TYNDALE
MOMENTUM®

*A Tyndale nonfiction imprint*

*To*
## BOB VERNON

*A man who loves books and great quotes . . .*
*A leader of men . . .*
*A tremendous friend!*

Visit Tyndale online at www.tyndale.com.

Visit Tyndale Momentum online at tyndalemomentum.com.

*Tyndale*, Tyndale's quill logo, *Tyndale Momentum*, and the Tyndale Momentum logo are registered trademarks of Tyndale House Ministries. Tyndale Momentum is a nonfiction imprint of Tyndale House Publishers, Carol Stream, Illinois.

*Phillips' Book of Great Thoughts and Funny Sayings*

For information about special discounts for bulk purchases, please contact Tyndale House Publishers at csresponse@tyndale.com, or call 1-855-277-9400.

**Library of Congress Cataloging-in-Publication Data**

A catalog record for this book is available from the Library of Congress.

ISBN 978-1-4964-8845-9

Printed in the United States of America

| 30 | 29 | 28 | 27 | 26 | 25 | 24 |
|----|----|----|----|----|----|----|
| 7  | 6  | 5  | 4  | 3  | 2  | 1  |

# Contents

vi

# A

ABILITY—AVERAGE

# ABILITY

What one cannot, another can.
*William Davenant*

The greatest ability in business is to get along with others and influence their actions.
*John Hancock*

There is no need to show your ability before everyone.
*Baltasar Gracian*

Everyone excels in something in which another fails.
*Latin proverb*

Executive ability is deciding quickly and getting somebody else to do the work.
*John G. Pollard*

They are able because they think they are able.
*Virgil*

It's pretty hard to be efficient without being obnoxious.
*Kin Hubbard*

# ABSENCE

Absence makes the heart grow fonder.
*T. H. Bayly*

Presents, I often say, endear absents.
*Charles Lamb*

The heart soon forgets what the eye sees not.

Out of sight, out of mind.
*Homer*

Absence diminishes little passions and increases great ones just as the wind blows out a candle and fans a fire.
*La Rochefoucauld*

The absent are always wrong.
*English proverb*

. . . that common cure of love.
*Miguel de Cervantes*

## ABSTINENCE

It is easier to abstain than to restrain.
*French proverb*

## ABSURDITY

There is nothing so absurd or ridiculous that has not at some time been said by some philosopher.
*Oliver Goldsmith*

## ABUNDANCE

Abundance, like want, ruins man.
*Benjamin Franklin*

## ACADEMIA

The average PhD thesis is nothing but the transference of bones from one graveyard to another.
*J. Frank Dobie*

## ACCIDENTS

The best insurance against car accidents is a Sunday afternoon nap.

After you've heard two eyewitness accounts of an auto accident, you begin to worry about history.

## ACCOMPLISHMENT

To accomplish great things, we must dream as well as act.
*Anatole France*

Who begins too much accomplishes little.
*German proverb*

## ACCOUNTANT

An accountant is a man hired to explain that you didn't make the money you did.

## ACCOUNTS

Budget: a mathematical confirmation of your suspicions.
*A. A. Latimer*

## ACCURACY

Even a stopped clock is right twice a day.
*Anonymous*

## ACCUSATION

Accuse: to affirm another's guilt or unworth; most commonly as a justification of ourselves for having wronged him.
*Ambrose Bierce*

## ACHIEVEMENT

Only those who dare to fail greatly can ever achieve greatly.
*Robert F. Kennedy*

I'm a slow walker, but I never walk back.
*Abraham Lincoln*

For a man to achieve all that is demanded of him he must regard himself as greater than he is.
*Johann Goethe*

When spider webs unite, they can tie up a lion.
*Ethiopian proverb*

Every calling is great when greatly pursued.
*Oliver Wendell Holmes Jr.*

Don't let what you cannot do interfere with what you can do.
*John Wooden*

The harder you work, the luckier you get.
*Gary Player*

There is no such thing as a great talent without great willpower.

Behold the turtle. He makes progress only when he sticks his neck out.
*James B. Conant*

Three great essentials to achieve anything worthwhile are, first, hard work; second, stick-to-itiveness; third, common sense.
*Thomas Edison*

## ACTING

Acting is a question of absorbing other people's personalities and adding some of your own experience.
*Paul Newman*

## ACTION

The shortest answer is doing.
*Lord Herbert*

Nothing will ever be attempted if all possible objections must be first overcome.
*Samuel Johnson*

I want to see you shoot the way you shout.
*Theodore Roosevelt*

I shall tell you a great secret, my friend. Do not wait for the last judgment; it takes place every day.
*Albert Camus*

Action takes precedence over study.
*Judah Hanasi*

Action is eloquence.
*William Shakespeare*

Action makes more fortunes than caution.
*Luc de Clapiers, Marquis de Vauvenargues*

Actions speak louder than words.

If a soldier or a labourer complains of the hardship of his lot, set him to do nothing.
*Blaise Pascal*

The way to get things done is not to mind who gets the credit of doing them.
*Benjamin Jowett*

If a thing is worth doing, it is worth doing badly.
*G. K. Chesterton*

The actions of men are the best interpreters of their thoughts.
*John Locke*

It is by acts and not by ideas that people live.
*Anatole France*

## ACTIVITY

Lose no time; be always employed in something useful.
*Benjamin Franklin*

Activity is contagious.
*Ralph Waldo Emerson*

## ACTOR

An actor is a guy who takes a girl in his arms, looks tenderly into her eyes, and tells her how great he is.

The only thing an actor fears more than losing his mind— is regaining it.

The one nice thing about actors—they don't go around talking about other people.

## ADMIRATION

Admiration is the daughter of ignorance.
*Benjamin Franklin*

Distance is a great promoter of admiration!
*Denis Diderot*

## ADOLESCENCE

Adolescence is that period when a young man can show you the best crop of hair he'll ever own.

Adolescence is the awkward age in the life of a youngster. They're too old for an allowance and too young for a credit card.

## ADULTS

A boy becomes an adult three years before his parents think he does . . . and about two years after he thinks he does.
*Lewis Hershey*

Adults are really not wiser than children; they're just more cunning.

## ADVANCEMENT

Build momentum by accumulating small successes.
*Anonymous*

I found that the men and women who got to the top were those who did the jobs they had in hand, with everything they had of energy and enthusiasm and hard work.
*Harry S. Truman*

## ADVENTURE

When you're safe at home you wish you were having an adventure; when you're having an adventure you wish you were safe at home.
*Thornton Wilder*

One does not discover new lands without consenting to lose sight of the shore for a very long time.
*André Gide*

## ADVERSITY

Man needs difficulties; they are necessary for health.
*Carl Jung*

In prosperity our friends know us; in adversity we know our friends.
*J. Churton Collins*

Misery acquaints a man with strange bedfellows.
*William Shakespeare*

Night brings our troubles to the light rather than banishes them.
*Seneca*

Trouble is only opportunity in work clothes.
*Henry J. Kaiser*

The man who is swimming against the stream knows the strength of it.
*Woodrow Wilson*

Great occasions do not make heroes or cowards; they simply unveil them to the eyes of men. Silently and imperceptibly, as we wake or sleep, we grow strong or weak; and at last some crisis shows what we have become.
*Brooke Foss Westcott*

Adversity has the same effect on a man that severe training has on the pugilist—it reduces him to his fighting weight.
*Josh Billings*

No untroubled day has ever dawned for me.
*Seneca*

They say a reasonable amount o' fleas is good for a dog— it keeps him from broodin' over bein' a dog mebbe.
*Edward Noyes Westcott*

I am escaped with the skin of my teeth.
*Job 19:20*

I never knew any man in my life who could not bear another's misfortunes perfectly like a Christian.
*Alexander Pope*

Every difficulty slurred over will be a ghost to disturb your repose later on.
*Frederic Chopin*

Adversity introduces a man to himself.
*Anonymous*

The diamond cannot be polished without friction, nor the man perfected without trials.
*Chinese proverb*

There is no education like adversity.
*Benjamin Disraeli*

When it is dark enough, men see the stars.
*Ralph Waldo Emerson*

Into each life some rain must fall.
*Henry W. Longfellow*

Our strength often increases in proportion to the obstacles which are imposed upon it.
*Rene Rapin*

Advise and counsel him; if he does not listen, let adversity teach him.
*Japanese proverb*

Adversity is the first path to truth.
*Lord Byron*

There is no education like adversity.
*Benjamin Disraeli*

Gold is tried by fire; brave men by adversity.
*Seneca*

The bravest sight in the world is to see a great man struggling against adversity.
*Seneca*

Adversity makes men, and prosperity makes monsters.
*Victor Hugo*

## ADVERTISING

Advertising helps raise the standard of living by raising the standard of longing.

Advertising encourages people to live beyond their means, but then, so does marriage.

Advertising is the rattling of a stick inside a swill bucket.
*George Orwell*

What kills a skunk is the publicity it gives itself.
*Abraham Lincoln*

Half the money I spend on advertising is wasted, and the trouble is, I don't know which half.
*John Wanamaker*

Give them quality. That's the best kind of advertising.
*Milton S. Hershey*

## ADVICE

Anybody can give advice—the trouble comes in finding someone interested in using it.

When we ask advice we are usually looking for an accomplice.

When a man asks you for advice, you can figure he isn't married.

Both medicine and advice are easy to prescribe but hard to take.

The best time to give advice to your children is while they're still young enough to believe you know what you're talking about.

Never give advice in a crowd.
*Arabian proverb*

Never trust the advice of a man in difficulties.
*Aesop*

Be frank and explicit. That is the right line to take when you wish to conceal your own mind and to confuse the minds of others.
*Benjamin Disraeli*

Advice is like snow; the softer it falls, the longer it dwells upon, and the deeper it sinks into the mind.
*Samuel Taylor Coleridge*

The true secret of giving advice is, after you have honestly given it, to be perfectly indifferent whether it is taken or not and never persist in trying to set people right.
*Hannah Whitall Smith*

Don't fight forces; use them.
*Buckminster Fuller*

People ask you for criticism, but they only want praise.
*W. Somerset Maugham*

He who builds to every man's advice will have a crooked house.
*Danish proverb*

Whatever advice you give, be brief.
*Horace*

Advice when most needed is least heeded.

In the multitude of counsellors there is safety.
*Proverbs 11:14*

Nothing is given so freely as advice.
*French proverb*

He that gives good advice, builds with one hand; he that gives good counsel and example, builds with both; but he that gives good admonition and bad example, builds with one hand and pulls down with the other.
*Francis Bacon*

## AFFLICTION

I thank God for my handicaps, for through them, I have found myself, my work, and my God.
*Helen Keller*

## AGE

Old age is when you find yourself using one bend-over to pick up two things.

By the time we learn to watch our step, we're not stepping out very much.

In youth the days are short and the years are long; in old age the years are short and the days long.
*Nikita Panin*

The first forty years of life give you the text; the next thirty supply the commentary on it.
*Arthur Schopenhauer*

When people tell you how young you look, they are also telling you how old you are.
*Cary Grant*

To be seventy years young is sometimes far more cheerful and hopeful than to be forty years old.
*Oliver Wendell Holmes*

How old would you be if you didn't know how old you was?
*Satchel Paige*

The tragedy of old age is not that one is old, but that one is young.
*Oscar Wilde*

The beauty of old men is the grey head.
*Proverbs 20:29*

Age is a sorry traveling companion.
*Danish proverb*

No one is so old as to think he cannot live one more year.
*Cicero*

When a woman tells you her age it's all right to look surprised, but don't scowl.
*Wilson Mizner*

If wrinkles must be written upon our brows, let them not be written upon the heart. The spirit should never grow old.
*James A. Garfield*

## AGGRESSIVENESS
The individual activity of one man with backbone will do more than a thousand men with a mere wishbone.
*J. H. Boetcher*

Not only strike while the iron is hot, but make it hot by striking.
*Oliver Cromwell*

You can't achieve anything without getting in someone's way.
*Abba Eban*

Whatsoever thy hand findeth to do, do it with thy might.
*Ecclesiastes 9:10*

## AGING
Nobody loves life like him who is growing old.
*Sophocles*

There are so few who can grow old with a good grace.
*Richard Steele*

When you were born, you cried and the world rejoiced. Live your life in such a manner that when you die, the world cries and you rejoice.

The worst thing, I fear, about being no longer young, is that one is no longer young.
*Harold Nicolson*

It is time to be old, to take in sail.
*Ralph Waldo Emerson*

Before you contradict an old man, my fair friend, you should endeavour to understand him.
*George Santayana*

Few people know how to be old.
*La Rochefoucauld*

I really believe that more harm is done by old men who cling to their influence than by young men who anticipate it.
*Owen D. Young*

A man over ninety is a great comfort to all his elderly neighbours: he is a picket-guard at the extreme outpost; and the young folks of sixty and seventy feel that the enemy must get by him before he can come near their camp.
*Oliver Wendell Holmes Jr.*

A person is always startled when he hears himself seriously called an old man for the first time.
*Oliver Wendell Holmes Jr.*

Age is a high price to pay for maturity.
*Tom Stoppard*

To know how to grow old is the master-work of wisdom, and one of the most difficult chapters in the great art of living.
*Henri Frederic Amiel*

When I was very young, I was disgracefully intolerant but when I passed the thirty mark I prided myself on having learned the beautiful lesson that all things were good, and equally good. That, however, was really laziness. Now, thank goodness, I've sorted out what matters and what doesn't. And I'm beginning to be intolerant again.
*G. B. Stern*

No wise man ever wished to be younger.
*Jonathan Swift*

I must be getting absent-minded. Whenever I complain that things aren't what they used to be, I always forget to include myself.
*George Burns*

Growing old—it's not nice, but it's interesting.
*August Strindberg*

They tell you that you'll lose your mind when you grow older. What they don't tell you is that you won't miss it very much.
*Malcolm Cowley*

## AGITATION

Those who profess to favor freedom, and yet depreciate agitation, are men who want rain without thunder and lightning. They want the ocean without the roar of its many waters.
*Frederick Douglass*

## AGREEMENT

I have never in my life learned anything from any man who agreed with me.
*Dudley Field Malone*

You may easily play a joke on a man who likes to argue— agree with him.
*Ed Howe*

## AGRICULTURE

Blessed be agriculture! If one does not have too much of it.
*Charles Dudley*

## AIR

The air is about the only remaining thing that's free, and it is becoming dangerous to breathe.

## AIR-CONDITIONING

The best thing about an air conditioner is that the neighbors can't borrow it.

## AIRPLANE

It will soon take only two hours to get around the world— one hour for the flying and one hour to get to the airport.

## AIRPORTS

It would have helped a lot if the pioneers had located cities closer to airports.

## ALARM CLOCKS

The only thing worse than hearing the alarm clock in the morning is not hearing it.

Some men have alarm clocks; I have my wife's elbow.

## ALLOWANCE

An allowance is what you pay your children to live with you.

## ALONE

Better to be alone than in bad company.

## AMATEURS

Show me an amateur and I'll show you a person who is always willing to give you the benefit of his inexperience.

## AMBITION

Ambition may be all right, but it sure can get a fellow into a lot of hard work.

When you are aspiring to the highest place, it is honorable to reach the second or even the third rank.
*Cicero*

Most people would succeed in small things if they were not troubled with great ambitions.
*Henry W. Longfellow*

I have no political ambitions for myself or my children.
*Joseph P. Kennedy*

The ripest peach is highest on the tree.
*James Whitcomb Riley*

I had ambition not only to go farther than any man had ever been before, but as far as it was possible for a man to go.
*Captain James Cook*

We grow small trying to be great.
*E. Stanley Jones*

Too low they build who build below the skies.
*Edward Young*

All ambitions are lawful except those which climb upward on the miseries or credulities of mankind.
*Joseph Conrad*

## AMERICA

America is one place where the people have complete control over how they pay their taxes—cash, check, or money order.

America is still the land of opportunity. Where else could you earn enough to owe so much?

Americanism means finding fault with other countries for not solving their problems while we wait without hope for the government to solve ours.

I only regret that I have but one life to lose for my country.
*Nathan Hale*

## AMERICANS

Americans are like a rich father who wishes he knew how to give his son the hardships that made him rich.
*Robert Frost*

## AMUSEMENT

I am a great friend to public amusements, for they keep people from vice.
*Samuel Johnson*

## ANCESTRY

I would rather make my name than inherit it.
*W. M. Thackeray*

I don't know who my grandfather was; I am much more concerned to know who his grandson will be.
*Abraham Lincoln*

## ANGER

Never answer a letter while you are angry.
*Chinese proverb*

It is easy to fly into a passion—anybody can do that—but to be angry with the right person to the right extent and at the right time and with the right object and in the right way— that is not easy, and it is not everyone who can do it.
*Aristotle*

Had Narcissus himself seen his own face when he had been angry, he could never have fallen in love with himself.
*Thomas Fuller*

An angry man opens his mouth and shuts up his eyes.
*Cato*

He that is slow to anger is better than the mighty; and he that ruleth his spirit than he that taketh a city.
*Proverbs 16:32*

Never go to bed mad. Stay up and fight.
*Phyllis Diller*

I never work better than when I am inspired by anger; for when I am angry, I can write, pray, and preach well, for then my whole temperament is quickened, my understanding sharpened, and all mundane vexations and temptations depart.
*Martin Luther*

An angry man stirreth up strife.
*Proverbs 29:22*

Anger is a better sign of the heart than of the head; it is a breaking out of the disease of honesty.
*Marquess of Halifax*

Anger is never sudden. It is born of a long, prior irritation that has ulcerated the spirit and built up an accumulation of force that results in an explosion. It follows that a fine outburst of rage is by no means a sign of a frank, direct nature.
*Cesare Pavese*

Anger resteth in the bosom of fools.
*Ecclesiastes 7:9*

Let not the sun go down upon your wrath.
*Ephesians 4:26*

Anger punishes itself.

Angry men seldom want woe.

Beware the fury of a patient man.
*John Dryden*

Anger is a bad counsellor.
*French proverb*

Anger renders the man insane and the prophet dumb.
*Hebrew proverb*

Anger manages everything badly.
*P. Statius*

However weak the hand, anger gives it strength.
*Ovid*

It is hidden wrath that harms.
*Seneca*

The greatest remedy for anger is delay.
*Seneca*

Anger is as a stone cast into a wasp's nest.
*Malabar proverb*

An angry man is again angry with himself when he returns to reason.
*Publilius Syrus*

Whenever you are angry, be assured that it is not only a present evil, but that you have increased a habit.
*Epictetus*

When a man is wrong and won't admit it, he always gets angry.
*Thomas Haliburton*

## ANIMALS
To his dog, every man is Napoleon; hence the constant popularity of dogs.
*Aldous Huxley*

## ANNIVERSARIES
The biggest surprise the average husband can give his wife on their anniversary is to remember it.

Many a man who misses an anniversary catches it later.

## ANSWERS

Answers are what we have for other people's problems.

No answer is also an answer.
*Danish proverb*

## ANTICIPATION

If pleasures are greatest in anticipation, just remember that this is also true of trouble.
*Elbert Hubbard*

A man's delight in looking forward to and hoping for some particular satisfaction is a part of the pleasure flowing out of it, enjoyed in advance. But this is afterward deducted, for the more we look forward to anything, the less we enjoy it when it comes.
*Arthur Schopenhauer*

We love to expect, and when expectation is either disappointed or gratified, we want to be again expecting.
*Samuel Johnson*

Nothing is so wretched or foolish as to anticipate misfortunes. What madness it is to be expecting evil before it comes.
*Seneca*

## ANTIPATHY

A cruel story runs on wheels, and every hand oils the wheels as they run.
*Louise Ouida*

The offender never pardons.
*George Herbert*

All the while thou studiest revenge, thou art tearing thy own wound open.

## ANTIQUES

Two kinds of families are likely to have a house full of antique furniture: the kind with money and the kind with children.

An antique is an object that has made a round trip to the attic.

If it is hard to dust, it's probably an antique.

One man's junk is another man's rare antique.

Antiques aren't always as old as they are cracked up to be.

## ANVIL

The anvil fears no blows.

## ANXIETY

Trouble is the common denominator of living. It is the great equalizer.
*Ann Landers*

Anxiety is a thin stream of fear trickling through the mind. If encouraged, it cuts a channel into which all other thoughts are drained.
*Arthur Somers Roche*

The thinner the ice, the more anxious is everyone to see whether it will bear.
*Josh Billings*

Where everything is bad, it must be good to know the worst.
*Francis H. Bradley*

We have a lot of anxieties, and one cancels out another very often.
*Winston Churchill*

God never built a Christian strong enough to carry today's duties and tomorrow's anxieties piled on the top of them.
*Theodore Ledyard Cuyler*

How much have cost us the evils that never happened!
*Thomas Jefferson*

Borrow trouble for yourself, if that's your nature, but don't lend it to your neighbors.
*Rudyard Kipling*

## APARTMENTS

An apartment building is a place where the landlord and the tenant are both trying to raise the rent.

I finally figured out how to make a landlord paint your apartment—move out.

The walls in my apartment are so thin that when I recently asked a visitor a question I got three answers.

## APATHY
One good thing about apathy is you don't have to exert yourself to show you're sincere about it.

## APHORISTS
Everything has been said before, but since nobody listens we have to keep going back and beginning all over again.
*André Gide*

Good things, when short, are twice as good.
*Baltasar Gracian*

Men's maxims reveal their characters.
*Marquis de Vauvenargues*

The only way to read a book of aphorisms without being bored is to open it at random and, having found something that interests you, close the book and meditate.
*Prince de Ligne*

Whatever sentence will bear to be read twice, we may be sure was thought twice.
*Henry David Thoreau*

Solomon made a book of proverbs, but a book of proverbs never made a Solomon.
*Anonymous*

All the good maxims already exist in the world; we just fail to apply them.
*Blaise Pascal*

## APOLOGIES
Never make a defence or apology before you be accused.
*King Charles I*

## APPEARANCE

All things are less dreadful than they seem.

Appearances are very deceitful.
*French proverb*

Things are not always what they seem.
*Phaedrus*

All that glitters is not gold.
*Miguel de Cervantes*

How little do they see what is, who frame their hasty judgments upon that which seems.
*Robert Southey*

You are only what you are when no one is looking.
*Robert C. Edwards*

The bosom can ache beneath diamond brooches; and many a blithe heart dances under coarse wool.
*Edwin Hubbel Chapin*

The proof of the pudding is in the eating, not in its looks.

Half the work that is done in this world is to make things appear what they are not.
*Elias Root Beadle*

There are no greater wretches in the world than many of those whom people in general take to be happy.
*Seneca*

## APPEASEMENT

Appeasers believe that if you keep on throwing steaks to a tiger, the tiger will turn vegetarian.
*Heywood Broun*

## APPETITE

He who cheats his appetite avoids debt.
*Chinese proverb*

A stomach that is seldom empty despises common food.
*Horace*

Seek an appetite by hard toil.
*Horace*

Always rise from the table with an appetite, and you will never sit down without one.
*William Penn*

The one thing bigger than my stomach is my appetite.

## APPLAUSE

The applause of the crowd makes the head giddy.
*Richard Steele*

## APPRECIATION

We never know the worth of water till the well is dry.
*English proverb*

I now perceive one immense omission in my Psychology— the deepest principle of Human Nature is the craving to be appreciated.
*William James*

## ARCHAEOLOGISTS

Archaeology is the science that proves you can't keep a good man down.

Show me an archaeologist, and I'll show you a man who practices skull drudgery.

## ARCHITECTURE

Architecture is frozen music.
*Johann Goethe*

## ARGUING

When arguing with a stupid person, be sure he isn't doing the same thing.

A man never tells you anything until you contradict him.
*George Bernard Shaw*

Between friends differences in taste or opinion are irritating in direct proportion to their triviality.
*W. H. Auden*

Silence is one of the hardest things to refute.
*Josh Billings*

A man convinced against his will is of the same opinion still.
*Samuel Butler*

A contentious man will never lack words.

Men may be convinced, but they cannot be pleased against their will.
*Samuel Johnson*

You have not converted a man because you have silenced him.

There are two sides to every question.
*Greek proverb*

A long dispute means both parties are wrong.
*Voltaire*

Any fact is better established by two or three good testimonies than by a thousand arguments.
*Nathaniel Emmons*

I learned long ago never to wrestle with a pig. You get dirty, and besides, the pig likes it.
*Cyrus Ching*

There is nothing so annoying as arguing with somebody who knows what he is talking about.

If you win all your arguments, you'll end up with no friends.

## ART
Art is poetry without words.
*Horace*

If my husband would ever meet a woman on the street who looked like the women in his paintings, he would fall over in a dead faint.
*Mrs. Pablo Picasso*

## ARTISTS
A modern artist is one who throws paint on a canvas, wipes it off with a cloth, and sells the cloth.

An artist cannot speak about his art any more than a plant can discuss horticulture.
*Jean Cocteau*

Every artist dips his brush in his own soul, and paints his own nature into his pictures.
*Henry Ward Beecher*

## ARTS
Real books should be the offspring not of daylight and casual talk but of darkness and silence.
*Marcel Proust*

## ASK
Do not ask a blind man which is the right way.
*German proverb*

Remember that in giving any reason at all for refusing, you lay some foundation for a future request.
*Arthur Helps*

## ASPIRATION
Make no little plans; they have no magic to stir men's blood. Make big plans, aim high in hope and work.
*Daniel H. Burnham*

'Tis but a base, ignoble mind that mounts no higher than a bird can soar.
*William Shakespeare*

In the long run men hit only what they aim at. Therefore, though they should fail immediately, they had better aim at something high.
*Henry David Thoreau*

## ASPIRIN
They now have a pill that's half aspirin and half glue. It's for people who get splitting headaches.

Aspirin is a miracle drug—a year's supply usually disappears in a month.

## ATHEISM

An atheist is a man who has no invisible means of support.

The trouble with atheism is that it has no future.

The fool hath said in his heart, There is no God.
*Psalm 14:1*

Nobody talks so constantly about God as those who insist that there is no God.
*Heywood Broun*

By night an atheist half-believes in God.
*Edward Young*

## ATTIC

Nobody who can read is ever successful at cleaning out the attic.

## ATTITUDE

Words can never adequately convey the incredible impact of our attitude toward life. The longer I live the more convinced I become that life is 10 percent what happens to us and 90 percent how we respond to it.
*Charles R. Swindoll*

This may shock you, but I believe the single most significant decision I can make on a day-to-day basis is my choice of attitude. It is more important than my past, my education, my bankroll, my successes or failures, fame or pain, what other people think of me or say about me, my circumstances, or my position. Attitude is that "single string" that keeps me going or cripples my progress. It alone fuels my fire or assaults my hope. When my attitudes are right, there's no barrier too high, no valley too deep, no dream too extreme, no challenge too great for me.
*Charles R. Swindoll*

To travel hopefully is better than to arrive.
*James Jeans*

Growl all day and you'll feel dog tired at night.
*Anonymous*

Instead of crying over spilt milk, go milk another cow.
*Erna Asp*

Life is a grindstone; whether it grinds you down or polishes
you up depends on what you're made of.
*Jacob M. Braude*

Poverty consists in feeling poor.
*Ralph Waldo Emerson*

Where there is an open mind, there will always be a frontier.
*Charles Kettering*

There are really only three types of people: those who make
things happen, those who watch things happen, and those
who say, What happened?
*Ann Landers*

Always imitate the behavior of the winners when you lose.
*George Meredith*

Your living is determined not so much by what life brings to
you as by the attitude you bring to life.
*John Homer Miller*

What we steadily, consciously, habitually think we are, that
we tend to become.
*John Cowper Powys*

Whenever you are asked if you can do a job, tell 'em,
Certainly, I can!—and get busy and find out how to do it.
*Theodore Roosevelt*

The people who get on in this world are the people who get
up and look for the circumstances they want and, if they can't
find them, make them.
*George Bernard Shaw*

As long as a man imagines that he cannot do a certain thing,
it is impossible for him to do it.
*Benedict Spinoza*

There is little difference in people . . . the little difference is
attitude. The big difference is whether it is positive or negative.
*Clement Stone*

We lost because we told ourselves we lost.
*Leo Tolstoy*

The world is full of cactus, but we don't have to sit on it.
*Will Foley*

## AUCTION

At an auction, keep your mouth shut.
*Spanish proverb*

## AUTHOR

The two most engaging powers on an author are to make new things familiar and familiar things new.
*W. M. Thackeray*

What moves men of genius, or rather, what inspires their work, is not new ideas, but their obsession with the idea that what has already been said is still not enough.
*Eugene Delacroix*

The mind conceives with pain, but brings forth with joy.
*Joseph Joubert*

It is as easy to dream a book as it is hard to write one.
*Honore Balzac*

There is no amount of praise which a man and an author cannot bear with equanimity. Some authors can even stand flattery.
*Maurice Baring*

No tears in the writer, no tears in the reader.

## AUTHORITY

If you wish to know what a man is, place him in authority.
*Yugoslav proverb*

## AUTOMATION

You cannot endow even the best machine with initiative.
*Walter Lippmann*

## AVAILABILITY
Most girls find that the one quality they admire the most in a man is availability.

## AVARICE
A covetous man does nothing well till he dies.

He who covets is always poor.
*Latin proverb*

## AVERAGE
I don't mind being average, because it means I'm as close to the top as I am to the bottom.

# B

BABY—BUY

## BABY

A loud noise at one end and no sense of responsibility at the other.
*Ronald Knox*

Every baby born into the world is a finer one than the last.
*Charles Dickens*

Feeding a baby is one sure way of finding out how badly your suit spots.

A soiled baby, with a neglected nose, cannot conscientiously be regarded as a thing of beauty.
*Mark Twain*

A baby is God's opinion that the world should go on.
*Carl Sandburg*

## BABY BOOMER

A Baby Boomer is a man who hires someone to cut the grass so he can play golf for the exercise.

## BACK FENCE

The back fence is the shortest distance between two gossips.

## BACKACHE

A backache is man's greatest labor-saving device.

## BAD

A bad reaper never gets a good sickle.
*Gaelic proverb*

## BAD LUCK

Bad luck is bending over to pick up a four-leaf clover and being infected by poison ivy.

## BALD

The big advantage of being bald is that you can style your hair with a damp cloth.

## BANKS

If money doesn't grow on trees, how come banks continue to sprout branches?

I know of a bank that is so big that they even have a special window for hold-ups.

Banks are peculiar institutions that urge you to save as much as possible of what you earn and urge you to borrow as much as you can spend, so you can spend more than you make.

It is easier to rob by setting up a bank than by holding up a bank clerk.
*Bertolt Brecht*

## BARGAINS

Today a bargain is anything that is only moderately overpriced.

"Bad, bad," says the buyer, but when he goes his way, then he boasts.
*Proverbs 20:14 (NASB)*

Necessity never made a good bargain.
*Benjamin Franklin*

Bargain: Something you can't use at a price you can't resist.
*Franklin P. Jones*

## BARK

Barking dogs seldom bite.

His bark is worse than his bite.

## BARS

Many a man goes into a bar for an eye-opener and comes out blind.

## BATH

My doctor told me to take a bath before retiring. But the way business is going, I won't be able to retire for twenty years.

## BATHROOM

The most frightening horror tales are those told by bathroom scales.

## BATHTUB

I'm using a square bathtub so I can't get a ring.

## BEAUTY

Beauty always comes from within—within jars, tubes, and compacts.

Beauty is power; a smile is its sword.
*Charles Reade*

Beauty and honesty seldom agree.

Beauty in distress is much the most affecting beauty.
*Edmund Burke*

Beauty without virtue is a flower without perfume.
*French proverb*

Beauty is a short-lived reign.
*Socrates*

Rare is the union of beauty and modesty.
*Juvenal*

## BED

Early to bed and early to rise is a sure sign that you're fed up with television.

As you make your bed, so you must lie on it.

Early to bed and early to rise,
Makes a man healthy, wealthy and wise.

## BEDLAM

Man has made his bedlam; let him lie in it.
*Fred Allen*

## BEES

We learn two lessons from the bees: one is not to be idle, and the other is not to get stung.

Honey is sweet, but the bee stings.

## BEGGING

Better to beg than steal, but better to work than beg.
*Russian proverb*

Beggars can't be choosers.

## BEGIN

Everything is difficult at first.
*Chinese proverb*

All glory comes from daring to begin.

Everything must have a beginning.

Good to begin well; better to end well.

He who begins many things, finishes but few.

The first step is as good as half over.

The beginning is half the whole.
*Greek proverb*

Well begun is half done.
*Horace*

Before beginning, prepare carefully.
*Cicero*

I start where the last man left off.
*Thomas Edison*

Begin it, and the work will be completed.
*Johann Goethe*

Once begun, a task is easy.
*Horace*

Great is the art of beginning, but greater is the art of ending.
*Henry W. Longfellow*

The beginning is the most important part of the work.
*Plato*

## BELIEF

Believe not all that you see nor half what you hear.

What a man desires he easily believes.

Seeing is believing.

Every man who attacks my belief diminishes in some degree
my confidence in it, and therefore makes me uneasy, and I am
angry with him who makes me uneasy.
*Samuel Johnson*

## BELLS

If you love not the noise of bells, why do you pull the ropes?

## BELLY

An empty belly hears nobody.

## BEND

Best to bend while it is a twig.

## BENEFIT

When befriended, remember it; when you befriend,
forget it.
*Benjamin Franklin*

Write injuries in dust, benefits in marble.

To accept a benefit is to sell one's freedom.
*Latin proverb*

If you stop to think about it, there are very few benefits in
your life for which you can take sole credit.
*Gary Smalley*

## BEST

The best things in life are free.

## BETRAYAL

This night, before the cock crow, thou shalt deny me thrice.
*Matthew 26:34*

Judas, betrayest thou the Son of man with a kiss?
*Luke 22:48*

## BETTER

Better a bare foot than none at all.

Better to wear out than to rust out.

## BEWARE

Beware of no man more than of thyself.

## BIBLE

Now that there's no more praying allowed in school, the kids may have to go to motels just to read a Bible.

All systems of morality are fine. The Gospel alone has exhibited a complete assemblage of the principles of morality, divested of all absurdity. It is not composed, like your creed, of a few commonplace sentences put into bad verse. Do you wish to see that which is really sublime? Repeat the Lord's Prayer.
*Napoleon Bonaparte*

It is impossible to govern the world without God and the Bible.
*George Washington*

The whole inspiration of our civilization springs from the teachings of Christ and the lessons of the prophets. To read the Bible for these fundamentals is a necessity of American life.
*Herbert Hoover*

In regard to this great book, I have but to say, it is the best gift God has given to man. All the good Savior gave to the world was communicated through this book. But for it we could not know right from wrong. All things most desirable for man's welfare, here and hereafter, are to be found portrayed in it.
*Abraham Lincoln*

A man has deprived himself of the best there is in the world who has deprived himself of this, a knowledge of the Bible. When you have read the Bible, you will know that it is the Word of God, because you will have found it the key to your own heart, your own happiness, and your own duty.
*Woodrow Wilson*

Hold fast to the Bible as the sheet-anchor of your liberties; write its precepts in your hearts and practice them in your lives. To the influence of this book we are indebted for all the progress made in true civilization, and to this we must look as our guide in the future. Righteousness exalteth a nation; but sin is a reproach to any people.
*Ulysses S. Grant*

There is no book like the Bible for excellent learning, wisdom, and use.
*Matthew Hale*

Thy word have I hid in mine heart, that I might not sin against thee.
*Psalm 119:11*

Every word of God is pure: he is a shield unto them that put their trust in him.
*Proverbs 30:5*

Man shall not live by bread alone, but by every word that proceedeth out of the mouth of God.
*Matthew 4:4*

There never was found, in any age of the world, either religion or law that did so highly exalt the public good as the Bible.
*Francis Bacon*

If we abide by the principles taught in the Bible, our country will go on prospering and to prosper; but if we and our posterity neglect its instructions and authority, no man can tell how sudden a catastrophe may overwhelm us and bury our glory in profound obscurity.
*Daniel Webster*

The Bible is worth all the other books which have ever been printed.
*Patrick Henry*

The Bible is a book in comparison with which all others in my eyes are of minor importance; and which in all my perplexities and distresses has never failed to give me light and strength.
*Robert E. Lee*

It was the Lord who put into my mind (I could feel His hand upon me) the fact that it would be possible to sail from here to the Indies. All who heard of my project rejected it with laughter, ridiculing me. There is no question that the inspiration was from the Holy Spirit, because He comforted me with rays of marvelous inspiration from the Holy Scriptures.
*Christopher Columbus*

The meaning of the Bible must be known and understood if it is to make a difference in our lives, and I urge all Americans to read and study the Scriptures. The rewards of such efforts will help preserve our heritage of freedom and signal the message of liberty to people in all lands.
*Ronald Reagan*

Every thinking man, when he thinks, realizes that the teachings of the Bible are so interwoven with our whole civic and social life that it would be literally impossible for us to figure what life would be if those teachings were removed. We would lose almost all the standards by which we now judge both public and private morals; all the standards towards which we, with more or less resolution, strive to raise ourselves.
*Theodore Roosevelt*

I have carefully and regularly perused these Holy Scriptures, and am of the opinion that the volume, independently of its divine origin, contains more true sublimity, more exquisite beauty, purer morality, more important history, and finer strains of poetry and eloquence, than could be collected within the same compass from all other books in whatever age or language they may have been written.
*William Jones*

I have made it a practice every year for several years to read through the Bible.
*John Adams*

In this age of space flight, when we use the modern tools of science to advance into new regions of human activity, the Bible . . . this grandiose, stirring history of the gradual revelation and unfolding of the moral law . . . remains in every way an up-to-date book. Our knowledge and use of the laws of nature that enable us to fly to the Moon also enable us to destroy our home planet with the atom bomb. Science itself does not address the question whether we should use the power at our disposal for good or for evil. The guidelines of what we ought to do are furnished in the moral law of God. It is no longer enough that we pray that God may be with us on our side. We must learn again to pray that we may be on God's side.
*Wernher von Braun*

I gleaned more practical psychology and psychiatry from the Bible than from all other books!
*George W. Crane*

So great is my veneration of the Bible that the earlier my children begin to read it the more confident will be my hope that they will prove useful citizens of their country and respectable members of society.
*John Adams*

America was born a Christian nation. America was born to exemplify that devotion to the elements of righteousness which are derived from the Holy Scriptures.
*Woodrow Wilson*

Our faith is not dependent upon human knowledge and scientific advance, but upon the unmistakable message of the Word of God.
*Billy Graham*

The Scriptures teach us the best way of living, the noblest way of suffering, and the most comfortable way of dying.
*Flavel*

The Bible goes equally to the cottage of the plain man and the palace of the king. It is woven into literature, and it colours the talk of the street. The bark of the merchant cannot sail to sea without it. No ship of war goes to conflict but the Bible is there. It enters men's closets; mingling in all grief and cheerfulness of life.
*Theodore Parker*

It is a belief in the Bible, the fruits of deep meditation, which has served me as the guide of my moral and literary life. I have found it a capital safely invested, and richly productive of interest.
*Johann Goethe*

The Bible is God's chart for you to steer by, to keep you from the bottom of the sea, and to show you where the harbor is, and how to reach it without running on rocks or bars.
*Henry Ward Beecher*

I don't think you can possibly grow up in an education in which the exposition of the life and the meaning of the life of Jesus is central, and not say that the New Testament is the most important book in your life, however much or little you may have in fact lived by it. It's the most powerful single volume you encounter.
*McGeorge Bundy*

It presents the unattainable standard of decency, or good behavior, or the moral life. Everybody has the problem of living with some kind of notion of what you ought to do, and those are the most powerful notions of ought that I've lived with.
*McGeorge Bundy*

I use the Scriptures, not as an arsenal to be resorted to only for arms and weapons, but as a matchless temple, where I delight to contemplate the beauty, the symmetry, and the magnificence of the structure, and to increase my awe and excite my devotion to the Deity there preached and adored.
*Boyle*

Thy word is a lamp unto my feet, and a light unto my path.
*Psalm 119:105*

I thoroughly believe in a university education for both men and women; but I believe a knowledge of the Bible without a college course is more valuable than a college course without the Bible.
*William Lyons Phelps*

## BID

Be not too hasty to outbid another.

## BILLS

Some people pay their bills when due, some when overdue, and some never do.

After looking at the bill for my operation, I understand why doctors wear masks in the operating room.

Maybe we can keep warm next winter by burning our bills.

Alas! How deeply painful is all payment!
*Lord Byron*

## BIOGRAPHY

You still shall live
(such virtue hath my pen)
Where breath most breathes
—even in the mouths of men.
*William Shakespeare*

## BIRD

Birds of a feather flock together.

The early bird catches the worm.

A bird in the hand is worth two in the bush.
*Greek proverb*

A bird is known by his feathers.
*Yiddish proverb*

## BIRTH

Show me a twin birth and I'll show you an infant replay.

## BLAME

He must be pure who would blame another.
*Danish proverb*

As long as we incorrectly blame outside sources for our miseries, it remains impossible to do much about them. However, if we realize that we upset ourselves over the things that happen to us, we can work at changing. The first step is to ask: Exactly how did I manage to upset myself? We then obtain the clues about how to avoid upsetting ourselves.
*Arnold Lazarus, Alan Fay*

## BLIND

Can the blind lead the blind? shall they not both fall into the ditch?
*Luke 6:39*

Better half blind than have both eyes out.

Folk ofttimes are most blind in their own cause.

None so blind as those who won't see.

When the blind man carries the banner, woe to those who follow.
*French proverb*

In the country of the blind, the one-eyed man is king.
*Erasmus*

## BLOWING

He that blows in the fire will get sparks in his eyes.
*German proverb*

## BOAST

Empty barrels make the most noise.

He that boasts of his own knowledge proclaims his ignorance.

Great boasters, little doers.
*French proverb*

Believe a boaster as you would a liar.
*Italian proverb*

## BODY

The spirit indeed is willing, but the flesh is weak.
*Matthew 26:41*

Alas, after a certain age, every man is responsible for his own face.
*Albert Camus*

The body says what words cannot.
*Martha Graham*

## BOLDNESS

In difficult situations the boldest plans are safest.
*Titus Livy*

Audacity augments courage.
*Publilius Syrus*

When you cannot make up your mind which of two evenly balanced courses of action you should take—choose the bolder.
*W. J. Slim*

## BOOK

When I am reading a book, whether wise or silly, it seems to me to be alive and talking to me.
*Jonathan Swift*

A drop of ink may make a million think.
*Lord Byron*

There are more books upon books than upon any other subject.
*Michel de Montaigne*

A good book contains more real wealth than a good bank.
*Roy L. Smith*

Books are the quietest and most constant of friends; they are the most accessible and wisest of counsellors, and the most patient of teachers.
*Charles W. Eliot*

Every great book is an action, and every great action is a book.
*Martin Luther*

A book may be as great a thing as a battle.
*Benjamin Disraeli*

That is a good book which is opened with expectation, and closed with profit.
*A. Bronson Alcott*

Books are ships which pass through the vast seas of time.
*Francis Bacon*

Judge not a book by its cover.

A room without books is like a body without a soul.
*Cicero*

Of making many books there is no end; and much study is a weariness of the flesh.
*Ecclesiastes 12:12*

It is from books that wise men derive consolation in the troubles of life.
*Victor Hugo*

Friends, books, a cheerful heart, and conscience clear are the most choice companions we have here.
*William Mather*

No matter what his rank or position may be, the lover of books is the richest and happiest of the children of men.
*John Alfred Langford*

Some good book is usually responsible for the success of every really great man.
*Roy L. Smith*

The real purpose of books is to trap the mind into doing its own thinking.
*Christopher Morley*

The first time I read an excellent book, it is to me just as if I had gained a new friend. When I read over a book I have perused before, it resembles the meeting with an old one.
*Oliver Goldsmith*

While you converse with lords and dukes, I have their betters here—my books.
*Thomas Sheridan*

You are the same today as you will be five years from now except for two things . . . the people you meet and the books you read.
*Charles E. Jones*

Except a living man, there is nothing more wonderful than a book!—a message to us from the dead—from human souls whom we never saw, who lived, perhaps, thousands of miles away; and yet these, in those little sheets of paper, speak to us, amuse us, terrify us, teach us, comfort us, open their hearts to us as brothers. . . . I say we ought to reverence books, to look at them as useful and mighty things. If they are good and true, whether they are about religion or politics, farming, trade, or medicine, they are the message of Christ, the maker of all things, the teacher of all truth.
*Charles Kingsley*

From the moment I picked up your book until I laid it down, I was convulsed with laughter. Some day I intend reading it.
*Groucho Marx*

Just the knowledge that a good book is awaiting one at the end of a long day makes that day happier.
*Kathleen Norris*

Do give books—religious or otherwise—for Christmas. They're never fattening, seldom sinful, and permanently personal.
*Lenore Hershey*

Book lovers never go to bed alone.
*Anonymous*

I read part of it all the way through.
*Sam Goldwyn*

A good book has no ending.
*R. D. Cumming*

No furniture is so charming as books.
*Sydney Smith*

One man is as good as another until he has written a book.
*Benjamin Jowett*

Where is human nature so weak as in the bookstore?
*Henry Ward Beecher*

To me the charm of an encyclopedia is that it knows—
and I needn't.
*Francis Yeats-Brown*

A good title is the title of a successful book.
*Raymond Chandler*

Some books are to be tasted, others to be swallowed, and some
few to be chewed and digested.
*Francis Bacon*

A book is like a garden carried in the pocket.
*Chinese proverb*

Books are the treasured wealth of the world and the fit
inheritance of generations and nations.
*Henry David Thoreau*

How many a man has dated a new era in his life from the
reading of a book.

## BORE

A yawn is nature's way of giving the person listening to a bore
an opportunity to open his mouth.

A bore is a man who deprives you of solitude without providing
you with company.
*Gian Vincenzo Gravina*

He has returned from Italy a greater bore than ever; he bores
on architecture, painting, statuary, and music.
*Sydney Smith*

We often forgive those who bore us, but can't forgive those
whom we bore.
*La Rochefoucauld*

A healthy male adult bore consumes, each year, one and a half
times his own weight in other people's patience.
*John Updike*

## BOREDOM

Boredom is . . . a vital consideration for the moralist, since at least half the sins of mankind are caused by the fear of it.
*Bertrand Russell*

Man is so unhappy that he would be bored even if he had no cause for boredom, by the very nature of his temperament, and he is so vain that, though he has a thousand and one basic reasons for being bored, the slightest thing, like pushing a ball with a billiard cue, will be enough to divert him.
*Blaise Pascal*

## BORROW

The borrower is servant to the lender.
*Proverbs 22:7*

Creditors have better memories than debtors.

He that goes a-borrowing goes a-sorrowing.

Borrowing is not much better than begging.
*German proverb*

Borrowing is the mother of trouble.
*Hebrew proverb*

He who does not have to borrow lives without cares.
*Yiddish proverb*

## BOW

Draw not your bow until your arrow is fixed.

## BOWLING

Interest your children in bowling—get them off the streets and into the alleys.

## BOY

Every boy who has a dog should also have a mother, so the dog can be fed regularly.

A boy becomes a man when he wears out the seat of his pants instead of the soles of his shoes.

Boys will be men one day.

When a boy is growing he has a wolf in his belly.
*German proverb*

Boys will be boys, and so will a lot of middle-aged men.
*Kin Hubbard*

## BRAGGING
One of the hardest things for most of us to put up with is a braggart who makes good.

## BRAIN
The brain is as strong as its weakest think.

He that hath a head of wax must not walk in the sun.

The only successful substitute for a lack of brains is silence.

## BREVITY
Brevity is the soul of wit.

If you would be pungent, be brief; for it is with words as with sunbeams—the more they are condensed, the deeper they burn.
*Robert Southey*

## BRIBE
Honesty stands at the gate and knocks, and bribery enters in.

## BRIDES
The father of the bride should realize he isn't losing a daughter but gaining a bathroom.

## BRIDGE
It's not a sin to play bridge, but it's a crime the way some people play it.

Bridge is a friendly game invented by two married couples who disliked each other.

One way to get a real kick out of bridge is to sit opposite your wife.

## BROOK

Before you drink at a brook, it is well to know its source.

## BUDGET

A budget is a system of reminding yourself that you can't afford the kind of living you've grown accustomed to.

A budget is a formula for determining that you need a raise.

A budget is a sort of conscience which doesn't keep you from spending, but makes you feel guilty about it.

The bureaucrats in Washington have finally figured out how to balance the budget—they're going to tilt the country.

Budgeting: A method of worrying before you spend instead of afterward.
*Anonymous*

## BUILD

The stone which the builders refused is become the head stone of the corner.
*Psalm 118:22*

## BULLY

A bully is always a coward.

## BURDEN

Every horse thinks his own pack heaviest.

None knows the weight of another's burden.

## BUREAUCRACY

The longer the title, the less important the job.
*George McGovern*

## BURGLARS

The best gift for the man who has everything is a burglar alarm.

Say what you will about burglars, they still make house calls.

## BUS

People are strange: they want the front of the bus, the back of the church, and the center of attention.

## BUSINESS

Business is so bad that even shoplifters have stopped coming.

I see where several of our politicians are predicting a return of prosperity as soon as business picks up.

If efficiency experts are so smart about running a business, how come they are always working for somebody else?

No nation was ever ruined by trade.
*Benjamin Franklin*

Whenever you see a successful business, someone once made a courageous decision.
*Peter Drucker*

One man's wage rise is another man's price increase.
*Harold Wilson*

Meetings are indispensable when you don't want to do anything.
*J. K. Galbraith*

A man isn't a man until he has to meet a payroll.
*Ivan Shaffer*

Invest in inflation. It's the only thing going up.
*Will Rogers*

If a cluttered desk is an indication of a cluttered mind, what is indicated by an empty desk?
*Anonymous*

The Middle East is a region where oil is thicker than blood.
*James Holland*

Along this tree
From root to crown
Ideas flow up
And vetoes down.
*Peter Drucker*

A company is judged by the president it keeps.
*James Hulbert*

The man who minds his own business usually has a good one.
*Anonymous*

Business? It's quite simple. It's other people's money.
*Alexander Dumas*

In the end, all business operations can be reduced to three words: people, product, and profits. People come first.
*Lee Iacocca*

It either is or ought to be evident to everyone that business has to prosper before anybody can get any benefit from it.
*Theodore Roosevelt*

Business is like riding a bicycle. Either you keep moving or you fall down.
*John David Wright*

Seest thou a man diligent in his business? he shall stand before kings.
*Proverbs 22:29*

A man without a smiling face must not open a shop.
*Chinese proverb*

Tell everybody your business and they will do it for you.
*Italian proverb*

The playthings of our elders are called business.
*St. Augustine*

Let every man mind his own business.
*Spanish proverb*

## BUSY
None so busy as those who do nothing.
*French proverb*

## BUY
There are more foolish buyers than foolish sellers.

The buyer needs a hundred eyes, the seller not one.
*Italian proverb*

Let the buyer beware.
*Latin proverb*

A study of economics usually reveals that the best time to buy anything is last year.
*Marty Allen*

Who buys has need of two eyes
But one's enough to sell the stuff.
*Anonymous*

What costs nothing is worth nothing.
*Anonymous*

People will buy anything that's one to a customer.
*Sinclair Lewis*

# C

CAKE—CURIOSITY

## CAKE

You can't eat your cake and have it too.

## CALAMITY

Calamity is the test of integrity.

## CALLING

You cannot choose your calling. Your calling chooses you. You have been blessed with special skills that are yours alone. Use them, whatever they may be, and forget about wearing another's hat. A talented chariot driver can win gold and renown with his skills. Let him pick figs and he would starve.
*Og Mandino*

## CANDLE

A candle lights others and consumes itself.

## CANDOR

Open rebuke is better than secret love.
*Proverbs 27:5*

There is no wisdom like frankness.
*Benjamin Disraeli*

## CAPITALISM

The capitalist system does not guarantee that everybody will become rich, but it guarantees that anybody can become rich.
*Raul R. de Sales*

## CARDS

The cards are ill shuffled till I have a good hand.
*Jonathan Swift*

## CAREER

Let him sing to the flute, who cannot sing to the harp.
*Cicero*

To find out what one is fitted to do and to secure an opportunity to do it is the key to happiness.
*John Dewey*

First, say to yourself what you would be; and then do what
you have to do.
*Epictetus*

Master a trade, and God will provide.
*Midrash*

## CARELESS
Throw not the child out with the bath.
*Danish proverb*

## CARS
If you would like to buy an $18,000 car it's easy—buy a $6,000
car on time.

## CASH
Nowadays you need a credit card to pay cash.

## CASTLE
Castles in the air cost a vast deal to keep up.

## CAT
When the cat's away, the mice will play.

If you play with a cat, you must not mind her scratch.
*Yiddish proverb*

## CAUSE
That cause is strong, which has not a multitude, but a strong
man behind it.
*James Russell Lowell*

No man is worth his salt who is not ready at all times to risk
his well-being, to risk his body, to risk his life, in a great cause.
*Theodore Roosevelt*

If you want to be an orator, first get your great cause.
*Wendell Phillips*

## CAUTION
No one tests the depth of a river with both feet.
*African proverb*

Caution, though often wasted, is a good risk to take.
*Josh Billings*

He who wants the rose must respect the thorn.
*Persian proverb*

Lock the stable door before the steed is stolen.

Hasten slowly.
*Augustus Caesar*

I don't like these cold, precise, perfect people, who, in order
not to speak wrong, never speak at all, and in order not to do
wrong, never do anything.
*Henry Ward Beecher*

Try the ice before you venture on it.

## CENSURE

It is folly for an eminent man to think of escaping censure,
and a weakness to be affected with it. All the illustrious
persons of antiquity, and indeed of every age in the world,
have passed through this fiery persecution.
*Joseph Addison*

## CERTAIN

Nothing is certain but death and taxes.
*Benjamin Franklin*

It is not certain that everything is uncertain.
*Blaise Pascal*

There is nothing certain in a man's life but that he must lose it.
*Owen Meredith*

## CHAIN

The chain is no stronger than its weakest link.

## CHANCE

Throw a lucky man into the sea, and he will come up with
a fish in his mouth.
*Arabian proverb*

## CHANGE

Progress is impossible without change; and those who cannot change their minds cannot change anything.
*George Bernard Shaw*

Change is not made without inconvenience, even from worse to better.
*Richard Hooker*

There is a certain relief in change, even though it be from bad to worse; as I have found in travelling in a stage-coach, that it is often a comfort to shift one's position and be bruised in a new place.
*Washington Irving*

Don't ever take a fence down until you know the reason why it was put up.
*G. K. Chesterton*

There is no way to make people like change. You can only make them feel less threatened by it.
*Frederick Hayes*

The world hates change, yet it is the only thing that has brought progress.
*Charles Kettering*

Who would be constant in happiness must often change.
*Chinese proverb*

The more it changes, the more it is the same thing.
*French proverb*

There is nothing permanent except change.
*Greek proverb*

Times change and we change with them.
*Latin proverb*

Everyone thinks of changing the world, but no one thinks of changing himself.
*Leo Tolstoy*

I've never met a person, I don't care what his condition, in whom I could not see possibilities. I don't care how much a man may consider himself a failure, I believe in him, for he can change the thing that is wrong in his life any time he is ready and prepared to do it. Whenever he develops the desire, he can take away from his life the thing that is defeating it. The capacity for reformation and change lies within.
*Preston Bradley*

## CHARACTER

You cannot make a crab walk straight.

What can you expect from a hog but a grunt.

The measure of a man's real character is what he would do if he knew he would never be found out.
*Lord Macaulay*

Character—the willingness to accept responsibility for one's own life—is the source from which self-respect springs.
*Joan Didion*

In matters of style, swim with the current; in matters of principle, stand like a rock.
*Thomas Jefferson*

Talents are best nurtured in solitude: character is best formed in the stormy billows of the world.
*Johann Goethe*

Everyone is a moon and has a dark side which he never shows to anybody.
*Mark Twain*

Character building begins in our infancy, and continues until death.
*Eleanor Roosevelt*

Character is a long-standing habit.
*Plutarch*

Moderation is an ostentatious proof of our strength of character.
*La Rochefoucauld*

If you think about what you ought to do for other people, your character will take care of itself.
*Woodrow Wilson*

You cannot dream yourself into a character; you must hammer and forge yourself one.
*James A. Froude*

Character is what God and the angels know of us; reputation is what men and women think of us.
*Horace Mann*

If you create an act, you create a habit. If you create a habit, you create a character. If you create a character, you create a destiny.
*Andre Maurois*

One can acquire everything in solitude except character.
*Stendhal*

If I take care of my character, my reputation will take care of itself.
*Dwight L. Moody*

Everyone ought to bear patiently the results of his own conduct.
*Phaedrus*

Every man has his follies—and often they are the most interesting things he has got.
*Josh Billings*

Learn to say "no"; it will be of more use to you than to be able to read Latin.
*Charles Haddon Spurgeon*

Every man in the world is better than some one else. And not as good as some one else.
*William Saroyan*

Listen to a man's words and look at the pupil of his eye. How can a man conceal his character?
*Mencius*

A man has no more character than he can command in a time of crisis.
*Ralph W. Sockmann*

Character is much easier kept than recovered.

Character is what you are in the dark.
*Dwight L. Moody*

A man shows his character by what he laughs at.
*German proverb*

Character is habit long continued.
*Greek proverb*

Good character is more to be praised than outstanding talent. Most talents are, to some extent, a gift. Good character, by contrast, is not given to us. We have to build it piece by piece—by thought, choice, courage, and determination.
*John Luther*

A man never discloses his own character so clearly as when he describes another's.
*Jean Paul Richter*

The four cornerstones of character on which the structure of this nation was built are: Initiative, Imagination, Individuality, and Independence.
*Edward Rickenbacker*

Instead of saying that man is the creature of circumstance, it would be nearer the mark to say that man is the architect of circumstance. It is character which builds an existence out of circumstance. From the same materials one man builds palaces, another hovels; one warehouses, another villas; bricks and mortar are mortar and bricks until the architect can make them something else.
*Thomas Carlyle*

## CHARITY

It is more blessed to give than to receive.
*Acts 20:35*

God loveth a cheerful giver.
*2 Corinthians 9:7*

He that hath pity upon the poor lendeth unto the LORD.
*Proverbs 19:17*

With malice toward none; with charity for all.
*Abraham Lincoln*

The biggest disease today is not leprosy or tuberculosis, but rather the feeling of being unwanted.
*Mother Teresa*

As the purse is emptied, the heart is filled.
*Victor Hugo*

He who waits to do a great deal of good at once, will never do anything.
*Samuel Johnson*

## CHASTITY

Who can find a virtuous woman? for her price is far above rubies.
*Proverbs 31:10*

## CHEAT

He that will cheat at play will cheat you any way.

## CHEERFULNESS

The sign of wisdom is a continual cheerfulness.
*French proverb*

I exhort you to be of good cheer.
*Acts 27:22*

A cheerful look makes a dish a feast.
*George Herbert*

The best way to cheer yourself up is to try to cheer somebody else up.
*Mark Twain*

Wondrous is the strength of cheerfulness, and its power of endurance—the cheerful man will do more in the same time, will do it better, will preserve it longer, than the sad or sullen.
*Thomas Carlyle*

The true source of cheerfulness is benevolence.
*P. Godwin*

Cheerfulness, in most cheerful people, is the rich and satisfying result of strenuous discipline.
*Edwin Percy Whipple*

Cheerfulness is the off-shoot of goodness.
*Christian Nestell Bovee*

## CHILDREN

Today, children of six seem to know all the questions and at sixteen they know all the answers.

There's one thing about children—they never go around showing snapshots of their grandparents.

If anything makes a child thirstier than going to bed, it's knowing that his parents have gone to bed too.

I've got two wonderful children—and two out of five isn't too bad.

My kid brother was sent from heaven—they must like it quiet up there.

One thing a child outgrows in a hurry is your pocketbook.

Better to be driven out from among men than to be disliked of children.
*Richard Henry Dana*

A wise son maketh a glad father.
*Proverbs 10:1*

Train up a child in the way he should go: and when he is old, he will not depart from it.
*Proverbs 22:6*

He followed in his father's footsteps, but his gait was somewhat erratic.
*Nicolas Bentley*

If children grew up according to early indications, we should have nothing but geniuses.
*Johann Goethe*

When I was a child, I spake as a child, I understood as a child, I thought as a child: but when I became a man, I put away childish things.
*1 Corinthians 13:11*

Children have never been very good at listening to their elders, but they have never failed to imitate them.
*James Baldwin*

Ask your child what he wants for dinner only if he is buying.
*Fran Lebowitz*

If a child lives with approval, he learns to live with himself.
*Dorothy Law Nolte*

What's done to children, they will do to society.
*Karl Menninger*

The hardest job kids face today is learning good manners without seeing any.
*Fred Astaire*

All children wear the sign: "I want to be important NOW." Many of our juvenile delinquency problems arise because nobody reads the sign.
*Dan Pursuit*

Children need love, especially when they do not deserve it.
*Harold S. Hulbert*

Suffer the little children to come unto me, and forbid them not; for of such is the kingdom of God.
*Mark 10:14*

Even a child is known by his doings.
*Proverbs 20:11*

A spoilt child never loves its mother.

Bachelors' wives and maids' children are well taught.

Children pick up words as pigeons peas.

Just as the twig is bent, the tree's inclined.
*Alexander Pope*

You can do anything with children if you only play with them.
*German proverb*

Childhood sometimes does pay a second visit to man; youth never.
*Anna Jameson*

My mother loved children—she would have given anything if I had been one.
*Groucho Marx*

## CHOICE
Regardless of circumstances, each man lives in a world of his own making.
*Josepha Murray Emms*

Between two evils, choose neither; between two goods, choose both.
*Tryon Edwards*

## CHRISTIANITY
Christian: one who believes that the New Testament is a divinely inspired book admirably suited to the spiritual needs of his neighbour.
*Ambrose Bierce*

Christianity is a battle, not a dream.
*Wendell Phillips*

The doctrine of the Kingdom of Heaven, which was the main teaching of Jesus, is certainly one of the most revolutionary doctrines that ever stirred and changed human thought.
*H. G. Wells*

## CHRISTMAS
Why does Christmas always come just when the stores are so crowded?

Show me an unemployed Santa, and I'll show you a ho-ho hobo!

Christmas is when you buy this year's gifts with next year's money.

## CHURCH

No sooner is a temple built to God, but the devil builds a chapel hard by.

## CHURCHGOING

America has become so tense and nervous, it has been years since I've seen anyone asleep in church—and that is a sad situation.
*Norman Vincent Peale*

Too hot to go to church? What about hell?
*Poster in Dayton, Ohio*

## CIRCUMSTANCE

The circumstances of others seem good to us, while ours seem good to others.
*Publilius Syrus*

Circumstances! I make circumstances!
*Napoleon Bonaparte*

## CITIZENSHIP

The first requisite of a good citizen in this republic of ours is that he should be able and willing to pull his weight.
*Theodore Roosevelt*

## CITY

Unless the LORD keep the city, the watchman waketh but in vain.
*Psalm 127:1*

## CIVILIZATION

You can't say civilization isn't advancing: in every war, they kill you in a new way.
*Will Rogers*

## CLERGYMAN

The defects of a preacher are soon spied.
*Martin Luther*

## COLD FEET

A lot of husbands suffer from cold feet, but not always their own.

## COMB

I got a pocket comb, but who wants to comb pockets?

## COMIC

A comic is a person, who, when he dies, is at his wit's end.

A comic is a man who originates old jokes.

## COMMITTEE

If you want to kill any idea in the world today, get a committee working on it.
*Charles F. Kettering*

## COMMON SENSE

Common sense is the knack of seeing things as they are, and doing things as they ought to be done.
*Calvin E. Stowe*

Common sense is not so common.
*French proverb*

## COMMUNICATION

Communication is depositing a part of yourself in another person.
*Anonymous*

## COMPANION

Birds of a feather flock together.

If you always live with those who are lame, you will yourself learn to limp.
*Latin proverb*

When a dove begins to associate with crows, its feathers remain white but its heart grows black.
*German proverb*

He is known by his companions.
*Latin proverb*

Tell me thy company and I will tell thee what thou art.
*Miguel de Cervantes*

He that walketh with wise men shall be wise.
*Proverbs 13:20*

## COMPANY
He that lies down with dogs will rise up with fleas.
*Latin proverb*

## COMPETITION
If you can't win, make the fellow ahead of you break the record.
*Anonymous*

He that wrestles with us strengthens our nerves and sharpens our skill. Our antagonist is our helper.
*Edmund Burke*

The competitor to be feared is one who never bothers about you at all, but goes on making his own business better all the time.
*Henry Ford Sr.*

Of all human powers operating on the affairs of mankind, none is greater than that of competition.
*Henry Clay*

I'm surprised how many people think you can throw a hand grenade at a competitor and expect he'll stand there and enjoy it.
*Frank Lorenzo*

## COMPLAINT
Depend upon it that if a man talks of his misfortunes there is something in them that is not disagreeable to him.
*Samuel Johnson*

Complaint is the largest tribute Heaven receives.
*Jonathan Swift*

## COMPLIMENT

Compliments cost nothing, yet many pay dearly for them.

A compliment is a gift, not to be thrown away carelessly unless you want to hurt the giver.
*Eleanor Hamilton*

You must not pay a person a compliment, and then straightway follow it with a criticism.
*Mark Twain*

A compliment is a forensic anaesthetic. Many people will complacently undergo a fatal interrogation if they be well flattered all the while; and more men are likely to be caught by a compliment to their ability than be a tribute to their virtue.
*Justice Darling*

I can live for two months on a good compliment.
*Mark Twain*

Some people pay a compliment as if they expected a receipt.
*Kin Hubbard*

## CONCEIT

Seest thou a man wise in his own conceit? There is more hope of a fool than of him.
*Proverbs 26:12*

He that falls in love with himself, will have no rivals.

## CONCENTRATION

Concentration is my motto—first honesty, then industry, then concentration.
*Andrew Carnegie*

## CONDUCT

Be swift to hear, slow to speak, slow to wrath.
*James 1:19*

Do not do unto others as you would that they should do unto you. Their tastes may not be the same.
*George Bernard Shaw*

# CONFESSION

Nothing spoils a confession like repentance.
*Anatole France*

The confession of evil works is the first beginning of good works.
*St. Augustine*

# CONFIDENCE

Doubt whom you will, but never yourself.
*Christian Nestell Bovee*

Men cannot be forced into trust.

If once you forfeit the confidence of your fellow citizen, you can never regain their respect and esteem.
*Abraham Lincoln*

# CONGRESS

They ran him for Congress. It was the best way to get him out of town.

You can lead a man to Congress, but you can't make him think.

Congress is where a man gets up to speak, says nothing, nobody listens—and then everybody disagrees.

# CONSCIENCE

Conscience is the inner voice that tells you the IRS might check your return.

Money talks louder when your conscience is asleep.

Conscience is an inner voice that warns us somebody is looking.

Conscience is the still small voice that makes you feel still smaller.

There is no pillow so soft as a clear conscience.
*French proverb*

A still small voice.
*1 Kings 19:12*

A good conscience is a continual feast.

A guilty conscience never thinks itself safe.

Conscience does make cowards of us all . . .
*William Shakespeare*

Keep conscience clear, then never fear.

There's no hell like a bad conscience.

The only tyrant I accept in this world is the still voice within.
*Mahatma Gandhi*

## CONTEMPLATION
He that contemplates on his bed hath a day without a night.

Night is the mother of thoughts.

## CONTENTMENT
He who is content can never be ruined.
*Chinese proverb*

A contented mind is a continual feast.

Better a little with content than much with contention.

The best of blessings—a contented mind.
*Latin proverb*

## CONTENTION
Religious contention is the devil's harvest.
*French proverb*

## CONTRACT
Remember, in every lease the big print giveth and the small print taketh away.
*Anonymous*

## CONVERSATION
The less men think; the more they talk.
*L. de Montesquieu*

Too much agreement kills a chat.
*Eldridge Cleaver*

Some persons talk simply because they think sound is more manageable than silence.
*Margaret Halsey*

If you can't say anything good about someone, sit right here by me.
*Alice Roosevelt Longworth*

A man's conversation is the mirror of his thoughts.
*Chinese proverb*

There are people who instead of listening to what is being said to them are already listening to what they are going to say themselves.
*Albert Guinon*

A timid question will always receive a confident answer.
*Justice Darling*

As long as a word remains unspoken, you are its master; once you utter it, you are its slave.
*Solomon Ibn Gabirol*

Say nothing good of yourself, you will be distrusted; say nothing bad of yourself, you will be taken at your word.
*Joseph Roux*

Conversation would be vastly improved by the constant use of four simple words: I do not know.
*André Maurois*

## CORRECTION
For whom the LORD loveth he correcteth.
*Proverbs 3:12*

## CORRESPONDENCE
As cold waters to a thirsty soul, so is good news from a far country.
*Proverbs 25:25*

## COST
What costs little is little esteemed.

## COST OF LIVING

Two can live as cheaply as one—if one doesn't eat.

## COUNTRY

Indeed I tremble for my country when I reflect that God is just.
*Thomas Jefferson*

## COURAGE

Courage is often just ignorance of the facts.

When moral courage feels that it is in the right, there is no personal daring of which it is incapable.
*Leigh Hunt*

Be on your guard; stand firm in the faith; be courageous; be strong.
*1 Corinthians 16:13 (NIV)*

There is no such thing as bravery; only degrees of fear.
*John Wainwright*

One man with courage is a majority.
*Andrew Jackson*

The first virtue in a soldier is endurance of fatigue; courage is only the second virtue.
*Napoleon Bonaparte*

Courage is fear holding on a minute longer.
*George S. Patton*

Valour lies just halfway between rashness and cowardice.
*Miguel de Cervantes*

Often the test of courage is not to die but to live.
*Vittorio Lafieri*

Courage is resistance to fear, mastery of fear—not absence of fear.
*Mark Twain*

A faint heart never won a fair lady.

The test of courage is to bear defeat without losing heart.

All are brave when the enemy flies.
*Italian proverb*

True courage is like a kite; a contrary wind raises it higher.
*J. Petit-Senn*

Last, but by no means least, courage—moral courage, the courage of one's convictions, the courage to see things through. The world is in a constant conspiracy against the brave. It's the age-old struggle—the roar of the crowd on one side and the voice of your conscience on the other.
*General Douglas MacArthur*

## COURT

The penalty for laughing in a courtroom is six months in jail; if it were not for this penalty, the jury would never hear the evidence.
*H. L. Mencken*

## COURTESY

Life is not so short but that there is always time enough for courtesy.
*Ralph Waldo Emerson*

There is not a single outward mark of courtesy that does not have a deep moral basis.
*Johann Goethe*

Politeness is the art of choosing among one's real thoughts.
*Abel Stevens*

Courtesy costs nothing.

To speak kindly does not hurt the tongue.

Intelligence and courtesy not always are combined; Often in a wooden house a golden room we find.
*Henry W. Longfellow*

## COWARD

To see what is right and not to do it is the part of a coward.
*Chinese proverb*

As cowardly as a coward is, it is not safe to call a coward a coward.
*Anonymous*

Cowards die many times before their deaths.
*William Shakespeare*

One coward makes ten.
*German proverb*

It is better to be the widow of a hero than the wife of a coward.
*Dolores Ibarruri*

The coward threatens when he is safe.
*Johann Goethe*

The valiant never taste of death but once.
*William Shakespeare*

## CREATION

In the beginning God created the heaven and the earth. And the earth was without form, and void; and darkness was upon the face of the deep. And the spirit of God moved upon the face of the waters. And God said, Let there be light: and there was light.
*Genesis 1:1-3*

## CREATIVITY

The creative mind plays with the objects it loves.
*Carl Jung*

## CREDIT

For the man who has everything, there is now a calendar to remind him when the payments are due.

He who sells on credit has much business but little cash.

The surest way to establish your credit is to work yourself into the position of not needing any.
*Maurice Switzer*

No man's credit is as good as his money.
*Ed Howe*

Nothing so cements and holds together all the parts of a society as faith or credit, which can never be kept up unless men are under some force or necessity of honestly paying what they owe to one another.
*Cicero*

Many people buy on time, but only few pay that way.

Credit cards: Due unto others.

## CREDULITY
Let us believe neither half of the good people tell us of ourselves, nor half the evil they say of others.
*J. Petit-Senn*

## CRIME
I was going to read the report about the rising crime rate— but somebody stole it.

These days there doesn't seem to be any arrest for the wicked.

We don't seem to be able to check crime, so why not legalize it and then tax it out of business.
*Will Rogers*

I have too great a soul to die like a criminal.
*John Wilkes Booth*

Set a thief to catch a thief.
*Anonymous*

Small crimes always precede great ones. Never have we seen timid innocence pass suddenly to extreme licentiousness.
*Jean Baptiste Racine*

## CRISIS
There can't be a crisis next week. My schedule is already full.
*Henry Kissinger*

Any idiot can face a crisis—it's this day-to-day living that wears you out.
*Anton Chekhov*

When written in Chinese the word *crisis* is composed of two characters. One represents danger and the other represents opportunity.
*John F. Kennedy*

Man is not imprisoned by habit. Great changes in him can be wrought by crisis—once that crisis can be recognized and understood.
*Norman Cousins*

## CRITIC

A critic is a legless man who teaches running.

A critic is a wet blanket that soaks everything it touches.

If you have no critics, you likely have no successes.
*Malcolm Forbes*

The critics arrived after the world was created.

He has a right to criticize, who has a heart to help.
*Abraham Lincoln*

## CRITICISM

Criticism wouldn't be so hard to take if it weren't so often right.

To avoid criticism, say nothing, do nothing, and be nothing.

Two things are bad for the heart—running upstairs and running down people.

Do not use a hatchet to remove a fly from your friend's forehead.

There's not the least thing can be said or done, but people will talk and find fault.
*Miguel de Cervantes*

Criticism is most effective when it sounds like praise.
*Arnold Glasow*

Criticism comes easier than craftsmanship.
*Zeuxis*

Blame-all and praise-all are two blockheads.

The sting of reproof is the truth of it.

Really to stop criticism one must die.
*French proverb*

The only impeccable writers are those that never wrote.
*William Hazlitt*

## CROSS
Everyone thinks his own cross is heaviest.
*Italian proverb*

## CROWD
Everyone in a crowd has the power to throw dirt: nine out of ten have the inclination.
*William Hazlitt*

## CRUELTY
All cruelty springs from weakness.
*Seneca*

## CRY
It is no use crying over spilled milk.

## CURE
What can't be cured must be endured.

## CURIOSITY
Curiosity is one of the permanent and certain characteristics of a vigorous intellect.
*Samuel Johnson*

The important thing is not to stop questioning.
*Albert Einstein*

No man really becomes a fool until he stops asking questions.
*Charles P. Steinmetz*

It is better to ask some of the questions than to know all the answers.
*James Thurber*

Too much curiosity lost Paradise.

Avoid a questioner, for he is also a tattler.
*Latin proverb*

# D

DANCING—DUTY

## DANCING

Dancing is a wonderful training for girls: it's the first way you learn to guess what a man is going to do before he does it.
*Christopher Morley*

Only an old-timer can remember when dancing was done with the feet.

## DANGER

A timid person is frightened before a danger, a coward during the time, and a courageous person afterwards.
*Jean Paul Richter*

Danger itself is the best remedy for danger.

He that would sail without danger must never come on the main sea.

Fear the goat from the front, the horse from the rear, and man from all sides.
*Russian proverb*

## DARKNESS

It is always darkest just before the day dawneth.
*Thomas Fuller*

## DAWN

When God sends the dawn, he sends it for all.
*Miguel de Cervantes*

## DAY

Boast not thyself of tomorrow; for thou knowest not what a day may bring forth.
*Proverbs 27:1*

Sufficient unto the day is the evil thereof.
*Matthew 6:34*

## DEAF

Blessed are the deaf, for they shall miss much idle gossip.

## DEATH

Death is nature's way of telling a man to slow down.

O death, where is thy sting? O grave, where is thy victory?
*1 Corinthians 15:55*

I have fought a good fight, I have finished my course, I have kept the faith.
*2 Timothy 4:7*

Cheerio, see you soon.

He has gone over to the majority.
*Petronius*

Most people would die sooner than think; in fact, they do.
*Bertrand Russell*

Death does not blow a trumpet.
*Danish proverb*

It is not death but dying which is terrible.

Six feet of earth make all equal.

No man should be afraid to die, who hath understood what it is to live.
*Thomas Fuller*

Oh well, no matter what happens, there's always death.
*Napoleon Bonaparte*

He that lives to forever, never fears dying.
*William Penn*

Truth sits upon the lips of dying men.
*Matthew Arnold*

## DEBT

Owe no man any thing, but to love one another.
*Romans 13:8*

A man in debt is caught in a net.

Out of debt, out of danger.

Never spend your money before you have it.
*Thomas Jefferson*

Some people use one half their ingenuity to get into debt, and the other half to avoid paying it.
*George D. Prentice*

## DECEIT

Let no man deceive you with vain words.
*Ephesians 5:6*

We are inclined to believe those whom we do not know because they have never deceived us.
*Samuel Johnson*

Some disguised deceits counterfeit truth so perfectly that not to be taken in by them would be an error of judgment.
*La Rochefoucauld*

If a man deceives me once, shame on him; if he deceives me twice, shame on me.

O what a tangled web we weave,
When first we practice to deceive!
*Walter Scott*

The easiest person to deceive is one's self.

The surest way to be deceived is to think one's self more clever than others.
*French proverb*

It is double pleasure to deceive the deceiver.
*Jean de la Fontaine*

All are not hunters that blow the horn.

All charming people have something to conceal, usually their total dependence on the appreciation of others.
*Cyril Connolly*

What we need is a rebirth of satire, of dissent, of irreverence, of an uncompromising insistence that phoniness is phony and platitudes are platitudinous.
*Arthur Schlesinger Jr.*

I have known a vast quantity of nonsense talked about bad men not looking you in the face. Don't trust that conventional idea. Dishonesty will stare honesty out of countenance, any day in the week, if there is anything to be got by it.
*Charles Dickens*

## DECISION-MAKING

A decision delayed until it is too late is not a decision; it's an evasion.
*Anonymous*

If I had to sum up in one word what makes a good manager, I'd say decisiveness.
*Lee Iacocca*

The percentage of mistakes in quick decisions is no greater than in long, drawn-out vacillations, and the effect of decisiveness itself "makes things go" and creates confidence.
*Anne O'Hare McCormick*

Problems come when the individual tries to hand over the decision making to a committee.
*Rupert Murdock*

Nothing is more difficult, and therefore more precious, than to be able to decide.
*Napoleon Bonaparte*

Once a decision was made, I did not worry about it afterward.
*Harry S Truman*

He who considers too much will perform little.
*German proverb*

I hate to see things done by halves. If it be right, do it boldly— if it be wrong, leave it undone.
*Bernard Gilpin*

When possible, make the decisions now, even if action is in the future. A reviewed decision usually is better than one reached at the last moment.
*William B. Given Jr.*

## DEEDS

Great things are done when men and mountains meet.
*William Blake*

Noble deeds that are concealed are most esteemed.
*Blaise Pascal*

Business is like a wheelbarrow—it stands still until someone pushes it.
*Anonymous*

If I cannot do great things, I can do small things in a great way.
*James F. Clarke*

It is not only what we do, but also what we do not do, for which we are accountable.
*Moliere*

No need of words; trust deeds.
*Ovid*

## DEFEAT

To lose is to learn.
*Anonymous*

There are some defeats more triumphant than victories.
*Michel de Montaigne*

## DEFENSE

Even the lion must defend himself against gnats.

The best defense is an offense.

## DELEGATE

As soon as a man climbs up to a high position, he must train his subordinates and trust them. They must relieve him of all small matters. He must be set free to think, to travel, to plan, to see important customers, to make improvements, to do all the big jobs of leadership.
*Herbert N. Casson*

No man is able of himself to do all things.
*Homer*

I leave everything to the young men. You've got to give youthful men authority and responsibility if you're going to build up an organization. Otherwise you'll always be the boss yourself and you won't leave anything behind you.
*Amadeo P. Giannini*

## DELIBERATION

If you think before you speak, the other fellow gets in his joke first.
*Ed Howe*

## DEMOCRACY

Democracy is based upon the conviction that there are extraordinary possibilities in ordinary people.
*Harry Emerson Fosdick*

The greatest blessing of our democracy is freedom. But in the last analysis, our only freedom is the freedom to discipline ourselves.
*Bernard Baruch*

What men value in the world is not rights, but privileges.
*H. L. Mencken*

The ballot is stronger than the bullet.
*Abraham Lincoln*

No man is good enough to govern another man without that other's consent.
*Abraham Lincoln*

Too many people expect wonders from democracy, when the most wonderful thing of all is just having it.
*Walter Winchell*

## DENTIST

I wish I had a dental appointment to cancel—it always brightens my day.

## DESIRE

It is much easier to suppress a first desire than to satisfy those that follow.
*La Rochefoucauld*

On the brink of being satiated, desire still appears infinite.
*Jean Rostand*

## DESPAIR

There is no vulture like despair.
*Lord Lansdowne*

## DESPOTISM

Dictators ride to and fro upon tigers which they dare not dismount. And the tigers are getting hungry.
*Winston Churchill*

## DESTINY

What are the thoughts of the canvas on which a masterpiece is being painted? "I am being soiled, brutally treated and concealed from view." Thus men grumble at their destiny, however fair.
*Jean Cocteau*

One meets his destiny often in the road he takes to avoid it.
*French proverb*

## DETAIL

Paying attention to simple little things that most men neglect makes a few men rich.
*Henry Ford Sr.*

## DETERMINATION

Every good and excellent thing stands moment by moment on the razor's edge of danger and must be fought for.
*Anonymous*

Do what you can, with what you have, where you are.
*Theodore Roosevelt*

It isn't the mountain ahead that wears you out—it's the grain of sand in your shoe.
*Robert Service*

Sink or swim.

## DEVIL

Resist the devil, and he will flee from you.
*James 4:7*

Every devil has not a cloven hoof.

Be sober, be vigilant; because your adversary the devil, as a roaring lion, walketh about, seeking whom he may devour.
*1 Peter 5:8*

The devil's boots don't creak.
*Scottish proverb*

One had as good eat the devil as the broth he's boiled in.

The devil sometimes speaks the truth.

The devil catches most souls in a golden net.
*German proverb*

He that is afraid of the devil does not grow rich.
*Italian proverb*

Talk of the devil and he'll appear.
*Latin proverb*

## DIAMOND

A diamond is a chunk of coal that made good under pressure.

A diamond is valuable tho' it lie on a dunghill.

## DICE

The best throw of the dice is to throw them away.

## DICTATION

The nicest thing about dictating a letter is that you can use words you don't know how to spell.

## DIE

Never say die.

## DIETING

I went on a fourteen-day diet, but all I lost was two weeks.

Minutes at the table don't put on weight—it's the seconds.

My doctor has the greatest diet of all: eat all you want, chew—but don't swallow.

If you cheat on your diet—you gain in the end.

The second day of a diet is always easier than the first—by the second day you're off it.

I told the doctor I get very tired when I go on a diet. So he gave me pep pills. You know what happened? I ate faster.

The one thing harder than sticking to a diet is keeping quiet about it.

Dieting is a way of starving to death so you can live longer.

Losing weight is a triumph of mind over platter.

## DIFFERENCE

Honest differences are often a healthy sign of progress.
*Mahatma Gandhi*

## DIFFICULTY

A smooth sea never made a skillful mariner.
*English proverb*

It is difficulties which show what men are.
*Epictetus*

There are no gains without pains.
*Benjamin Franklin*

All things are difficult before they are easy.
*Thomas Fuller*

I sometimes suspect that half our difficulties are imaginary and that if we kept quiet about them, they would disappear.
*Robert Lynd*

Difficulty is the daughter of idleness.

What is worthwhile must needs be difficult.
*Latin proverb*

Difficulties are meant to rouse, not discourage. The human spirit is to grow strong by conflict.
*William Ellery Channing*

## DIGNITY

There is a healthful hardiness about real dignity that never dreads contact and communion with others, however humble.
*Washington Irving*

## DILEMMA

. . . Between the devil and the deep sea.

. . . Between the hammer and the anvil.
*Latin proverb*

## DILIGENCE

The diligent hand maketh rich.

The diligent spinner has a large shift.

Diligence is the mother of good luck.
*Benjamin Franklin*

Few things are impossible to diligence and skill. . . . Great works are performed, not by strength, but perseverance.
*Samuel Johnson*

## DINING

It isn't so much what's on the table that matters as what's on the chairs.
*W. S. Gilbert*

## DIRECTION

Trust in the LORD with all thine heart; and lean not unto thine own understanding. In all thy ways acknowledge him, and he shall direct thy paths.
*Proverbs 3:5-6*

## DISAPPOINTMENT

Nothing is so good as it seems beforehand.

Disappointment is the nurse of wisdom.
*Boyle Roche*

Too many people miss the silver lining because they're expecting gold.
*Maurice Scitter*

## DISASTERS

Calamities are of two kinds: misfortune to ourselves, and good fortune to others.
*Ambrose Bierce*

## DISC JOCKEYS

Radio news is bearable. This is due to the fact that while the news is being broadcast the disc jockey is not allowed to talk.
*Fran Lebowitz*

## DISCONTENTMENT

Let thy discontents be thy secrets.

## DISCOURAGEMENT

It's a rare person who doesn't get discouraged. Whether it happens to us or to an associate we're trying to cheer up, the answer centers around one word: perseverance.

## DISCOVERY

If I have ever made any valuable discoveries, it has been owing more to patient attention, than to any other talent.
*Isaac Newton*

## DISCRETION

It is not good to wake a sleeping lion.
*Philip Sidney*

A lean compromise is better than a fat lawsuit.

As a jewel of gold in a swine's snout, so is a fair woman which is without discretion.
*Proverbs 11:22*

An ounce of discretion is worth a pound of wit.

Nothing is more dangerous than a friend without discretion;
even a prudent enemy is preferable.
*Jean de la Fontaine*

I have never been hurt by anything I didn't say.
*Calvin Coolidge*

## DISCUSSION
Discussion is the anvil on which the spark of truth is struck.

## DISEASE
Feed a cold and starve a fever.

Illness makes a man a scoundrel.
*Samuel Johnson*

The beginning of health is to know the disease.
*Spanish proverb*

Some remedies are worse than the diseases.
*Publilius Syrus*

## DISGRACE
Better not live at all than live disgraced.
*Greek proverb*

## DISLIKE
I do desire we may be better strangers.
*William Shakespeare*

## DISPUTE
There is no disputing about tastes.
*Latin proverb*

## DISSENT
Thought that is silenced is always rebellious. . . . Majorities,
of course, are often mistaken. This is why the silencing of
minorities is always dangerous. Criticism and dissent are the
indispensable antidote to major delusions.
*Alan Barth*

## DISTANCE
Respect is greater from a distance.
*Latin proverb*

## DISTRUST
Doubt the man who swears to his devotion.
*Louise Colet*

What loneliness is more lonely than distrust?
*George Eliot*

Distrust is poison to friendship.

Never trust a man who speaks well of everybody.
*John Churton Collins*

## DIVIDE
He who divides honey with the bear gets the lesser share.
*Italian proverb*

## DIVORCE
All that's needed for a divorce today is a wedding.

There are three chief causes of divorce in America—men, women, and marriage.

## DOCTORS
My son is thinking of becoming a doctor. He has the handwriting for it.

Doctors have been classified into three types—expensive, costly, and exorbitant.

Some doctors tell their patients the worst—others mail them the bill.

My doctor saved my life once. I called him to the house and he never showed up.

The best doctor is the one you run for and can't find.
*Denis Diderot*

The person most often late for a doctor's appointment is the doctor himself.

One doctor makes work for another.

Wherever a doctor cannot do good, he must be kept from doing harm.
*Hippocrates*

A man who is his own doctor has a fool for his patient.

Every doctor has his favorite disease.

God heals and the doctor takes the fee.

The doctor is more to be feared than the disease.
*French proverb*

Doctors think a lot of patients are cured who have simply quit in disgust.
*Don Herold*

## DOCTRINE
In religion as in politics, it so happens that we have less charity for those who believe half our creed than for those who deny the whole of it.
*Walter Colton*

## DOGS
Every dog has his day—but the nights are reserved for the cats.

A dog teaches a boy fidelity, perseverance, and to turn around three times before lying down.
*Robert Benchley*

If you can't bite, don't show your teeth.
*Yiddish proverb*

The dog is turned to his own vomit again.
*2 Peter 2:22*

If you wish the dog to follow you, feed him.

It is hard to teach an old dog new tricks.

Let sleeping dogs lie.

Beware of a silent dog and still water.
*Latin proverb*

## DOING

It is easier to know how to do than it is to do.
*Chinese proverb*

Do as I say, not as I do.

Do what you ought and come what can.

No man can do nothing and no man can do everything.
*German proverb*

What is done cannot be undone.
*Italian proverb*

To do two things at once is to do neither.
*Latin proverb*

Whatever you do, do with all your might.
*Latin proverb*

We become just by performing just actions, temperate by performing temperate actions, brave by performing brave actions.
*Aristotle*

Whatsoever thy hand findeth to do, do it with thy might; for there is no work, nor device, nor knowledge, nor wisdom, in the grave, whither thou goest.
*Ecclesiastes 9:10*

Men are all alike in their promises. It is only in their deeds that they differ.
*Moliere*

No one knows what he can do till he tries.
*Publilius Syrus*

## DOLLAR

Nowadays, a dollar saved is a quarter earned.

## DOUBT

He who knows nothing doubts nothing.
*French proverb*

To believe with certainty, we must begin with doubting.
*Stanislaw I, king of Poland*

## DREAM

To make your dream come true, you have to stay awake.

Last night I got a double rest. I dreamed I was sleeping.

A dreamer is a person who goes through life having a wonderful time spending money he hasn't got.

Some men see things as they are and ask why. I dream things that never were and say, why not?
*George Bernard Shaw*

All men of action are dreamers.
*James G. Huneker*

The Future is something which everyone reaches at the rate of sixty minutes an hour, whatever he does, whoever he is.
*C. S. Lewis*

## DRESS

No fine clothes can hide the clown.

It is an interesting question how far men would retain their relative rank if they were divested of their clothes.
*Henry David Thoreau*

## DRINK

A hot drink is as good as an overcoat.
*Latin proverb*

## DRINKING

One of the disadvantages of wine is that it makes a man mistake words for thoughts.
*Samuel Johnson*

Woe unto them that rise up early in the morning, that they may follow strong drink.
*Isaiah 5:11*

Much drinking, little thinking.

O God! That men should put any enemy in their mouths to steal away their brains.
*William Shakespeare*

The drunkard's joy is the sober man's woe.

What the sober man thinks, the drunkard tells.
*French proverb*

## DRIVING

Nothing improves a man's driving like the sudden discovery
that his license has expired.

## DROP

The whole ocean is made up of little drops.

Drop by drop fills the tub.
*French proverb*

## DROWN

A drowning man will catch at a straw.

A drowning man will catch on to the edge of a sword.
*Yiddish proverb*

## DULLNESS

Sir, he was dull in company, dull in his closet, dull everywhere.
He was dull in a new way, and that made people think him
great.
*Samuel Johnson*

He is not only dull in himself, but the cause of dullness in
others.
*Samuel Foote*

## DUTY

Do your duty in all things. You could not do more. You would
not wish to do less.
*Robert E. Lee*

Duty before pleasure.

Duty determines destiny.

God never imposes a duty without giving the time to perform it.

In doing what we ought we deserve no praise.
*Latin proverb*

Do something every day that you don't want to do; this is the golden rule for acquiring the habit of doing your duty without pain.
*Mark Twain*

Let us do our duty in our shop or our kitchen, in the market, the street, the office, the school, the home, just as faithfully as if we stood in the front rank of some great battle and knew that victory for mankind depended on our bravery, strength, and skill. When we do that, the humblest of us will be serving in that great army which achieves the welfare of the world.
*Theodore Parker*

Never mind your happiness; do your duty.
*Will Durant*

For strength to bear is found in duty alone, and he is blest indeed who learns to make the joy of others cure his own heartache.
*Drake*

# E

EAR—EYE

## EAR

One pair of ears draws a hundred tongues.

The ear is the road to the heart.
*French proverb*

We have two ears and one mouth that we may listen the more and talk the less.
*Greek proverb*

## EATING

Whether therefore ye eat, or drink, or whatsoever ye do, do all to the glory of God.
*1 Corinthians 10:31*

The way to a man's heart is through his stomach.

Better is a dinner of herbs where love is, than a stalled ox and hatred therewith.
*Proverbs 15:17*

Part of the secret of success in life is to eat what you like and let the food fight it out inside.
*Mark Twain*

## EAVESDROPPING

He who listens at doors hears much more than he likes.

## EDUCATION

A self-taught man usually has a poor teacher and a worse student.

The schools ain't what they used to be and never was.
*Will Rogers*

Surely the shortest commencement address in history—and for me one of the most memorable—was that of Dr. Harold E. Hyde, president of New Hampshire's Plymouth State College. He reduced his message to the graduating class to these three ideals: "Know yourself—Socrates. Control yourself—Cicero. Give yourself—Christ."
*Walter T. Tatara*

Educate a man and you educate an individual—educate a woman and you educate a family.
*Agnes Cripps*

There is that indescribable freshness and unconsciousness about an illiterate person that humbles and mocks the power of the noblest expressive genius.
*Walt Whitman*

Intelligence appears to be the thing that enables a man to get along without education. Education appears to be the thing that enables a man to get along without the use of his intelligence.
*A. E. Wiggan*

No one can become really educated without having pursued some study in which he took no interest. For it is part of education to interest ourselves in subjects for which we have no aptitude.
*T. S. Eliot*

Nothing in education is so astonishing as the amount of ignorance it accumulates in the form of inert facts.
*Henry Adams*

Perhaps the most valuable result of all education is the ability to make yourself do the thing you have to do, when it ought to be done, whether you like it or not; it is the first lesson that ought to be learned, and however early a man's training begins, it is probably the last lesson that he learns thoroughly.
*Thomas Huxley*

Education is the ability to listen to almost anything without losing your temper or your self-confidence.
*Robert Frost*

We must reject that most dismal and fatuous notion that education is a preparation for life.
*Northrop Frye*

The Romans would never have had time to conquer the world if they had been obliged to learn Latin first of all.
*Heinrich Heine*

The ultimate goal of the educational system is to shift to the individual the burden of pursuing his education.
*John W. Gardner*

Fathers send their sons to college either because they went to college, or because they didn't.
*L. L. Hendren*

All learning has an emotional base.
*Plato*

Whatever is good to know is difficult to learn.
*Greek proverb*

If you think education is expensive—try ignorance.
*Derek Bok*

It is the studying that you do after your school days that really counts. Otherwise you know only that which everyone else knows.
*Henry L. Doherty*

The purpose of education is to teach oneself how to study on their own.
*R. E. Phillips*

Educate men without religion and you make them but clever devils.
*Duke of Wellington*

Education makes people easy to lead, but difficult to drive; easy to govern, but impossible to enslave.
*Henry Peter Brougham*

## EFFORT

Any supervisor worth his salt would rather deal with people who attempt too much than with those who try too little.
*Lee Iacocca*

It is hard to fail, but it is worse never to have tried to succeed. In this life we get nothing save by effort.
*Theodore Roosevelt*

## EGG

Put all your eggs in one basket—and watch the basket.
*Mark Twain*

He who treads on eggs must tread lightly.
*German proverb*

He that would have eggs must endure the cackling of hens.
*Latin proverb*

## EGO

He who is full of himself is likely to be quite empty.

When a man tries himself, the verdict is in his favor.

Talk to a man about himself and he will listen for hours.
*Benjamin Disraeli*

When a man is wrapped up in himself, he makes a very small package.

## ELOQUENCE

The finest eloquence is that which gets things done; the worst is that which delays them.

To say that he was not at a loss for a word is one of the great understatements of all time. He was not at a loss for 500,000 words and we heard 'em, every one.
*William Connor*

## EMBARRASSMENT

We never forgive those who make us blush.

A stitch in time saves embarrassing exposure.

Nothing is so embarrassing as watching your boss do something you told him couldn't be done.

An embarrassing moment is spitting out of a car window when it's not open.

## EMOTION

When dealing with people, remember you are not dealing with creatures of logic, but with creatures of emotion, creatures bristling with prejudice, and motivated by pride and vanity.
*Dale Carnegie*

By starving emotions we become humorless, rigid and stereotyped; by repressing them we become literal, reformatory and holier-than-thou; encouraged, they perfume life; discouraged, they poison it.
*Joseph Collins*

It is easier to manufacture seven facts out of whole cloth than one emotion.
*Mark Twain*

## EMPLOYEE RELATIONS

Much outcry, little outcome.
*Aesop*

Few men ever drop dead from overwork, but many quietly curl up and die because of undersatisfaction.
*Sydney Harris*

Respect a man, he will do the more.
*James Howell*

Don't mind anything that anyone tells you about anyone else. Judge everyone and everything for yourself.
*Henry James*

The art of being wise is the art of knowing what to overlook.
*William James*

Never discourage anyone who continually makes progress, no matter how slow.
*Plato*

A smile in giving honest criticism can make the difference between resentment and reform.
*Philip Steinmetz*

## ENEMIES

A wise man gets more use from his enemies than a fool from his friends.
*Baltasar Gracian*

He that wrestles with us strengthens our nerves, and sharpens our skill. Our antagonist is our helper.
*Edmund Burke*

Don't think there are no crocodiles because the water is calm.
*Malayan proverb*

You can discover what your enemy fears most by observing the means he uses to frighten you.
*Eric Hoffer*

The space in a needle's eye is sufficient for two friends, but the whole world is scarcely big enough to hold two enemies.
*Solomon Ibn Gabirol*

There's nothing like the sight of an old enemy down on his luck.
*Euripides*

Love your enemies.
*Matthew 5:44*

Enemies are so stimulating.
*Katharine Hepburn*

To have a good enemy, choose a friend: he knows where to strike.
*Diane de Poitiers*

I choose my friends for their good looks, my acquaintances for their good characters, and my enemies for their intellects. A man cannot be too careful in the choice of his enemies.
*Oscar Wilde*

Speak well of your enemies, sir, you made them.
*Oren Arnold*

Nothing ever perplexes an adversary so much as an appeal to his honour.
*Benjamin Disraeli*

You have many enemies that know not why they are so, but, like to village-curs, bark when their fellows do.
*William Shakespeare*

Man is his own worst enemy.
*Cicero*

If thine enemy be hungry, give him bread to eat.
*Proverbs 25:21*

A man's greatness can be measured by his enemy.

Love your enemies, for they tell you your faults.
*Benjamin Franklin*

Even from a foe a man may learn wisdom.
*Greek proverb*

His must be a very wretched fortune who has no enemy.
*Latin proverb*

Observe your enemies, for they first find out your faults.
*Antisthenes*

Everyone needs a warm personal enemy or two to keep him free from rust in the movable parts of his mind.
*Gene Fowler*

Nothing would more contribute to make a man wise than to have always an enemy in his view.
*Lord Halifax*

## ENTHUSIASM

Enthusiasm is the greatest asset in the world. It beats money and power and influence.
*Henry Chester*

If you want to be enthusiastic, act enthusiastic. Inner enthusiasm follows.
*William Ellis*

The simplest man, fired with enthusiasm, is more persuasive than the most eloquent man without it.
*Franklin Field*

In things pertaining to enthusiasm, no man is sane who does not know how to be insane on proper occasions.
*Henry Ward Beecher*

The worst bankrupt in the world is the man who has lost his enthusiasm.
*H. W. Arnold*
Enthusiasm is the highest paid quality on earth.
*Frank Bettger*

No person who is enthusiastic about his work has anything to fear from life.
*Samuel Goldwyn*

## ENVY

Envy is the sincerest form of flattery.

As rust corrupts iron, so envy corrupts man.
*Greek proverb*

Envy is a kind of praise.
*John Gay*

## EPITAPH

What I gave, I have; what I spent, I had; what I kept, I lost.

Reading the epitaphs, our only salvation lies in resurrecting the dead and burying the living.
*Paul Eldridge*

The only real equality is in the cemetery.
*German proverb*

## EQUALITY

We hold these truths to be self-evident: that all men are created equal; that they are endowed by their Creator with inalienable rights; that among these are life, liberty and the pursuit of happiness.
*Thomas Jefferson*

## ERROR

It takes less time to do a thing right than it does to explain why you did it wrong.
*Henry W. Longfellow*

## ESCAPE

Oh that I had wings like a dove! For then would I fly away,
and be at rest.
*Psalm 55:6*

## ETHICS

It is easier to fight for one's principles than to live up to them.
*Alfred Adler*

## ETIQUETTE

Etiquette is the art of knowing the right way to do a wrong
thing.

## EVIDENCE

By their fruits ye shall know them.
*Matthew 7:20*

## EVIL

Woe unto them that call evil good, and good evil.
*Isaiah 5:20*

To great evils we submit; we resent little provocations.
*William Hazlitt*

Be not overcome of evil, but overcome evil with good.
*Romans 12:21*

I had rather be a doorkeeper in the house of my God,
than to dwell in the tents of wickedness.
*Psalm 84:10*

Men loved darkness rather than light, because their deeds
were evil.
*John 3:19*

For the wages of sin is death.
*Romans 6:23*

Of two evils choose the least.

All men are evil and will declare themselves to be so when
occasion is offered.
*Sir Walter Raleigh*

I never wonder to see men wicked, but I often wonder to see them not ashamed.
*Jonathan Swift*

Evil often triumphs, but never conquers.
*Joseph Roux*

A person may cause evil to others not only by his actions but by his inaction, and in either case he is justly accountable to them for the injury.
*John Stuart Mill*

Evil unchecked grows, evil tolerated poisons the whole system.
*Jawaharlal Nehru*

## EXAGGERATION

We always weaken whatever we exaggerate.
*Jean François de Laharpe*

There are people so addicted to exaggeration they can't tell the truth without lying.
*Josh Billings*

## EXAMPLE

Example is the greatest of all seducers.
*French proverb*

There is nothing more contagious than a bad example.
*French proverb*

The first great gift we can bestow on others is a good example.
*Thomas Morell*

## EXCELLENCE

Excellence in any art or profession is attained only by hard and persistent work.
*Theodore Martin*

## EXCEPTIONS

Why does everyone think he is an exception to the rules?

# EXCUSES

Two wrongs don't make a right, but they make a good excuse.
*Thomas Szasz*

A person who is going to commit an inhuman act invariably excuses himself by saying, "I'm only human, after all."
*Sydney J. Harris*

An excuse is worse and more terrible than a lie; for an excuse is a lie guarded.
*Alexander Pope*

# EXECUTIVE

The best executive is the one who has sense enough to pick good men to do what he wants done, and self-restraint enough to keep from meddling with them while they do it.
*Theodore Roosevelt*

# EXERCISE

To exercise is human; not to is divine.
*Robert Orben*

After dinner, rest a while, after supper walk a mile.
*Arabian proverb*

I like long walks, especially when they are taken by people who annoy me.
*Fred Allen*

If you don't find time to exercise, you'll have to find time for illness.

# EXISTENCE

The individual who has to justify his existence by his own efforts is in eternal bondage to himself.
*Eric Hoffer*

# EXPECTATION

Blessed is he who expects nothing, for he shall never be disappointed.

## EXPENSES

Beware of little expenses: A small leak will sink a great ship.
*Benjamin Franklin*

Meeting your expenses is easy—in fact, it's impossible to avoid them.

## EXPERIENCE

Experience teaches best because it gives you individual instruction.

Experience enables you to recognize a mistake when you make it again.

Experience is what's left after you've lost everything else.

You acquire experience in one of two ways: by doing, or by being done.

Experience is what you get while you are looking for something else.

Experience is what happens to you while you are making other plans.

Deep experience is never peaceful.
*Henry James*

Experience is the name so many people give to their mistakes.
*Oscar Wilde*

A proverb is no proverb to you till life has illustrated it.
*John Keats*

Everything happens to everybody sooner or later if there is time enough.
*George Bernard Shaw*

Good judgment comes from experience, and experience—well, that comes from poor judgment.
*Anonymous*

You cannot create experience. You must undergo it.
*Albert Camus*

The more sand has escaped from the hourglass of our life,
the clearer we should see through it.

*Jean Paul Sartre*

He returns wisest that comes home whipt with his own follies.

Once bit, twice shy.

## EXPERT

Make three correct guesses consecutively and you will establish
a reputation as an expert.

*Lawrence Peter*

## EXTRAVAGANCE

He who buys what he needs not, sells what he needs.

*Japanese proverb*

## EYE

An eye can threaten like a loaded and levelled gun, or it can
insult like hissing or kicking; or, in its altered mood, by beams
of kindness, it can make the heart dance for joy.

*Ralph Waldo Emerson*

# F

FACE—FUTURE

## FACE

Men's faces are not to be trusted.
*Latin proverb*

Often a silent face has voice and words.
*Latin proverb*

The face is the portrait of the mind; the eyes, its informers.
*Latin proverb*

The tartness of his face sours ripe grapes.
*William Shakespeare*

At fifty everyone has the face he deserves.
*George Orwell*

## FACTS

Let us keep our mouths shut and our pens dry until we know the facts.
*Anton J. Carlson*

## FAILURE

Show me a thoroughly satisfied man—and I will show you a failure.
*Thomas Edison*

Half the failures in life arise from pulling in one's horse as he is leaping.
*Julius Charles Hare*

The line between failure and success is so fine that we scarcely know when we pass it; so fine that we are often on the line and do not know it.
*Elbert Hubbard*

He who never fails will never grow rich.

There is not a fiercer hell than the failure in a great object.
*John Keats*

I cannot give you the formula for success, but I can give you the formula for failure—which is: Try to please everybody.
*Herbert B. Swope*

There are two kinds of men who never amount to much:
Those who cannot do what they are told, and those who can
do nothing else.
*Cyrus H. Curtis*

He was a self-made man who owed his lack of success to
nobody.
*Joseph Heller*

Everyone pushes a falling fence.
*Chinese proverb*

Ninety-nine percent of failures come from people who have
the habit of making excuses.
*George Washington Carver*

## FAIR-WEATHER FRIEND
A fair-weather friend is one who is always around when he
needs you.

## FAITH
We walk by faith, not by sight.
*2 Corinthians 5:7*

Now faith is the substance of things hoped for, the evidence
of things not seen.
*Hebrews 11:1*

Faith without works is dead.
*James 2:26*

The just shall live by faith.
*Romans 1:17*

Philosophic argument, especially that drawn from the vastness
of the universe, in comparison with the apparent insignificance
of this globe, has sometimes shaken my reason for the faith
that is in me; but my heart has always assured and reassured
me that the gospel of Jesus Christ must be Divine Reality. The
Sermon on the Mount cannot be a mere human production.
This belief enters into the very depth of my conscience. The
whole history of man proves it.
*Daniel Webster*

I have fought a good fight, I have finished my course, I have kept the faith.
*2 Timothy 4:7*

## FALL

Let him that thinketh he standeth take heed lest he fall.
*1 Corinthians 10:12*

## FALLIBILITY

Even the youngest of us may be wrong sometimes.
*George Bernard Shaw*

## FAME

If you would not be forgotten as soon as you are dead, either write things worth reading or do things worth writing.
*Benjamin Franklin*

Fame can never make us lie down contentedly on a deathbed.
*Alexander Pope*

Fame is a vapour, popularity an accident; the only earthly certainty is oblivion.
*Mark Twain*

No true and permanent fame can be found except in labors which promote the happiness of mankind.
*Charles Sumner*

What a heavy burden is a name that has become too famous.
*Voltaire*

Fame usually comes to those who are thinking about something else.
*Oliver Wendell Holmes Jr.*

The final test of fame is to have a crazy person imagine he is you.
*Anonymous*

All celebrated people lose dignity on a close view.
*Napoleon Bonaparte*

Famous remarks are very seldom quoted correctly.
*Simeon Strunsky*

Fame is a bee
It has a song—
It has a sting—
Ah, too, it has a wing.
*Emily Dickinson*

Fame is but wind.

Fame is proof that people are gullible.
*Ralph Waldo Emerson*

We are so presumptuous that we should like to be known all over the world, even by people who will only come when we are no more. Such is our vanity that the good opinion of half a dozen of the people around us gives us pleasure and satisfaction.
*Blaise Pascal*

Wealth is like sea-water; the more we drink, the thirstier we become; and the same is true of fame.
*Arthur Schopenhauer*

Fame is so sweet that we love anything with which we connect it, even death.
*Blaise Pascal*

Men are rewarded and punished not for what they do, but rather for how their acts are defined. This is why men are more interested in better justifying themselves than in better behaving themselves.
*Thomas Szasz*

There are persons who, when they cease to shock us, cease to interest us.
*F. H. Bradley*

Those are most desirous of honour and glory who cry out loudest at its abuse and the vanity of the world.
*Baruch Spinoza*

## FAMILIARITY

Though familiarity may not breed contempt, it takes off the edge of admiration.
*William Hazlitt*

# FAMILY

Every family tree always produces nuts.

A guest never knows how much to laugh at a family joke.

The best part of some family trees is underground.

I put a mirror on my TV set. I wanted to see what my family looked like.

Who of us is mature enough for offspring before the offspring themselves arrive? The value of marriage is not that adults produce children but that children produce adults.
*Peter de Vries*

No matter how many communes anybody invents, the family always creeps back.
*Margaret Mead*

Happy families are all alike; every unhappy family is unhappy in its own way.
*Leo Tolstoy*

God gives us relatives; thank God we can choose our friends.
*A. Mizner*

He that flies from his own family has far to travel.
*Latin proverb*

What the mother sings to the cradle goes all the way down to the coffin.
*Henry Ward Beecher*

I advise thee to visit thy relations and friends; but I advise thee not to live too near to them.
*Thomas Fuller*

If you cannot get rid of the family skeleton, you may as well make it dance.
*George Bernard Shaw*

A family is a unit composed not only of children but of men, women, an occasional animal, and the common cold.
*Ogden Nash*

## FANATICS

The worst of madmen is a saint run mad.
*Alexander Pope*

## FAREWELLS

Laughter is not at all a bad beginning for a friendship, and it is far the best ending for one.
*Oscar Wilde*

It is amazing how nice people are to you when they know you are going away.
*Michael Arlen*

## FASHION

Be not the first by whom the new are tried,
Nor yet the last to lay the old aside.
*Alexander Pope*

It is not only fine feathers that make fine birds.
*Aesop*

## FATHER

The skin you love to touch: Dad's old pigskin wallet.

Like father, like son.

## FATHER'S DAY

Last Father's Day my son gave me something I've always wanted—the keys to my car.

## FAULT

A fault confessed is half redressed.

If a friend tell thee a fault, imagine always that he telleth thee not the whole.
*Thomas Fuller*

His shortcoming is his long staying.
*Anonymous*

A fault once denied is twice committed.

People say ill-natured things without design, but not without having a pleasure in them.
*William Hazlitt*

Faults are thick where love is thin.

The first faults are theirs that commit them; the second theirs that permit them.

Those who live in glass houses should not throw stones.

The fault of another is a good teacher.
*German proverb*

Love him who tells you your faults in private.
*Hebrew proverb*

People who have no faults are terrible; there is no way of taking advantage of them.
*Anatole France*

If we had no faults we should not take so much pleasure in noticing them in others.
*La Rochefoucauld*

There are persons who always find a hair in their plate of soup for the simple reason that, when they sit down before it, they shake their heads until one falls in.
*Friedrich Hebbel*

## FAVORS
When some men discharge an obligation, you can hear the report for miles around.
*Mark Twain*

## FEAR
Fear is not an unknown emotion to us.
*Neil Armstrong*

How does one kill fear, I wonder? How do you shoot a spectre through the heart, slash off its spectral head, take it by the spectral throat?
*Joseph Conrad*

The suspense is terrible. I hope it will last.
*Oscar Wilde*

In grief we know the worst of what we feel, but who can tell the end of what we fear?
*Hannah More*

I would often be a coward, but for the shame of it.
*Ralph Connor*

Fear is the father of courage and the mother of safety.

Courage is often caused by fear.
*French proverb*

## FIDELITY

It is better to be faithful than famous.
*Theodore Roosevelt*

Drink waters out of thine own cistern.
*Proverbs 5:15*

## FINANCE

Alexander Hamilton originated the put and take system in our national treasury: the taxpayers put it in, and the politicians take it out.
*Will Rogers*

## FIRE

He that would have fire must bear with smoke.
*Dutch proverb*

The fire which warms us at a distance will burn us when near.

Out of the frying pan into the fire.
*Tertullian*

There is no smoke without fire.
*Latin proverb*

## FIRMNESS

The purpose firm is equal to the deed.
*Edward Young*

## FIRST

First come, first served.

## FISH

Fish are supposed to be brain food, and yet people eat it on Friday and then do the silliest things over the weekend.

## FISHING

The only time a fisherman tells the truth is when he calls another fisherman a liar.

Unfortunately, fish seem to go on vacation the same time we do.

## FIT

If the cap fits, wear it.

## FLAT

As flat as a pancake.

## FLATTERY

It is easy to flatter; it is hard to praise.
*Jean Paul Richter*

A man that flattereth his neighbour spreadeth a net for his feet.
*Proverbs 29:5*

Flattery corrupts both the receiver and the giver.

Flattery is like cologne water, to be smelt of, not swallowed.

When flatterers meet, the devil goes to dinner.

One catches more flies with a spoonful of honey than with twenty casks of vinegar.
*French proverb*

Blarney is flattery laid on so thin you love it; baloney is flattery laid on so thick you hate it.
*Fulton Sheen*

Just praise is only a debt, but flattery is a present.
*Samuel Johnson*

## FLIRTATION

It is the same in love as in war; a fortress that parleys is half taken.
*Marguerite De Valois*

## FLOWERS

Where flowers degenerate man cannot live.
*Napoleon Bonaparte*

## FLIES

A shut mouth catches no flies.
*Spanish proverb*

## FOOD

The only food that doesn't go up in price is food for thought.

Lips, however rosy, must be fed.

Dinner, a time when . . . one would eat wisely but not too well, and talk well but not too wisely.
*W. Somerset Maugham*

A hungry man is not a free man.
*Adlai Stevenson*

A great step toward independence is a good-humoured stomach.
*Seneca*

If you wish to grow thinner, diminish your dinner.
*H. S. Leigh*

Hunger is the best sauce.

A smiling face is half the meal.
*Latvian proverb*

Gluttony is an emotional escape, a sign something is eating us.
*Peter de Vries*

Some people have a foolish way of not minding, or pretending not to mind, what they eat. For my part, I mind my belly very studiously, and very carefully; for I look upon it, that he who does not mind his belly will hardly mind anything else.
*Samuel Johnson*

# FOOL

Most fools think they are only ignorant.
*Benjamin Franklin*

A fool's mouth is his destruction.
*Proverbs 18:7*

As a dog returneth to his vomit, so a fool returneth to his folly.
*Proverbs 26:11*

Even a fool, when he holdeth his peace, is counted wise.
*Proverbs 17:28*

Let a person meet a bear robbed of her cubs, rather than a fool in his foolishness.
*Proverbs 17:12 (NASB)*

The way of a fool is right in his own eyes.
*Proverbs 12:15*

A fool and his money are soon parted.

No fool like an old fool.

To reprove a fool is but labor lost.

A fool says what he knows, and a wise man knows what he says.
*Yiddish proverb*

A fool who can keep silent is counted among the wise.
*Yiddish proverb*

A fool can no more see his own folly than he can see his ears.
*William Thackeray*

Lord, what fools these mortals be!
*William Shakespeare*

A learned fool is more foolish than an ignorant fool.
*Moliere*

There are two kinds of fools: One says, "This is old, therefore it is good"; the other says, "This is new, therefore it is better."
*William R. Inge*

Nothing is more humiliating than to see idiots succeed in enterprises we have failed in.
*Gustave Flaubert*

Fools never open their mouths without subtracting from the sum of human knowledge.

However big the fool, there is always a bigger fool to admire him.

Whenever a man does a thoroughly stupid thing, it is always from the noblest motives.
*Oscar Wilde*

## FORCE

Force and not opinion is the queen of the world; but it is opinion that uses the force.
*Blaise Pascal*

Who overcomes by force overcomes but half his foe.

You may lead a horse to water but you can't make him drink.

## FORESIGHT

If only our foresight were as good as our hindsight!

## FORGET

It is sometimes expedient to forget even what you know.
*Latin proverb*

## FORGIVE

Forgive us our debts, as we forgive our debtors.
*Matthew 6:12*

Nobody ever forgets where he buried a hatchet.
*Kin Hubbard*

Only the brave know how to forgive.

One pardons in the degree that one loves.
*La Rochefoucauld*

To understand is to forgive.
*French proverb*

Know all and you will pardon all.
*Greek proverb*

To forgive everyone is as much cruelty as to forgive no one.
*Greek proverb*

Don't carry a grudge. While you're carrying the grudge the other guy's out dancing.
*Buddy Hackett*

The weak can never forgive. Forgiveness is the attribute of the strong.
*Mahatma Gandhi*

## FORTUNE

Fortune makes him fool, whom she makes her darling.
*Francis Bacon*

Fortune truly helps those who are of good judgment.
*Euripides*

Men are seldom blessed with good fortune and good sense at the same time.
*Titus Livy*

Great fortune brings with it great misfortune.

He that waits upon fortune is never sure of a dinner.

Greater qualities are needed to bear good fortune than bad.
*French proverb*

Fortune and misfortune are neighbors.
*German proverb*

## FOX

A fox should not be on the jury at a goose's trial.
*Thomas Fuller*

The fox barks not when he would steal the lamb.

## FREEDOM

The cause of freedom is the cause of God.
*Samuel Bowles*

Personal liberty is the paramount essential to human dignity and human happiness.
*Edward Bulwer-Lytton*

Since the general civilizations of mankind I believe there are more instances of the abridgment of the freedom of the people by gradual and silent encroachments of those in power than by violent and sudden usurpations.
*James Madison*

The condition upon which God has given liberty to man is eternal vigilance.
*John Philpot Curran*

The sweetest freedom is an honest heart.

Man is free at the moment he wishes to be.
*Voltaire*

He who has lost his freedom has nothing else to lose.
*German proverb*

The cost of freedom is always high, but Americans have always paid it. And one path we shall never choose, and that is the path of surrender, or submission.
*John F. Kennedy*

## FREE SPEECH

Some people's idea of [free speech] is that they are free to say what they like, but if anyone says anything back, that is an outrage.
*Winston Churchill*

The most stringent protection of free speech would not protect a man from falsely shouting fire in a theater and causing a panic.
*Oliver Wendell Holmes Jr.*

## FRIEND

I misplaced our Christmas list. Now I haven't the slightest idea who our friends are.

The best way to lose a friend is to tell him something for his own good.

Faithful are the wounds of a friend, but the kisses of an enemy are deceitful.
*Proverbs 27:6 (NKJV)*

Iron sharpeneth iron; so a man sharpeneth the countenance of his friend.
*Proverbs 27:17*

To a friend's house the road is never long.
*Dutch proverb*

A friend is never known till he is needed.

A man dies as often as he loses his friends.
*Francis Bacon*

Prosperity makes friends and adversity tries them. A true friend is one soul in two bodies.
*Aristotle*

Chance makes our parents, but choice makes our friends.
*Jacques Delille*

I am wealthy in my friends.
*William Shakespeare*

A friend must not be injured, even in jest.
*Publilius Syrus*

He makes no friend who never made a foe.
*Alfred, Lord Tennyson*

A friend in power is a friend lost.
*Henry Adams*

In life it is difficult to say who does you the most mischief, enemies with the worst intentions, or friends with the best.
*Edward Bulwer-Lytton*

Don't tell your friends their social faults; they will cure the fault and never forgive you.
*Logan Pearsall Smith*

One friend in a life is much, two are many, three are hardly possible.
*Henry Brooks Adams*

Friends agree best at a distance.

He is a good friend that speaks well of me behind my back.

My son, keep well thy tongue, and keep thy friend.
*Chaucer*

Promises may get friends, but performance must keep them.

The only way to have a friend is to be one.

Friends have all things in common.
*Greek proverb*

Make new friends, but don't forget the old ones.
*Yiddish proverb*

Enemies publish themselves. They declare war. The friend never declares his love.
*Henry David Thoreau*

We have fewer friends than we imagine, but more than we know.
*Hugo von Hofmannsthal*

It is more shameful to distrust one's friends than to be deceived by them.
*La Rochefoucauld*

It is not so much our friends' help that helps us as the confident knowledge that they will help us.
*Epicurus*

It is easier to forgive an enemy than to forgive a friend.
*William Blake*

So long as we are loved by others I should say that we are almost indispensable; and no man is useless while he has a friend.
*Robert Louis Stevenson*

A friend is a gift you give yourself.
*Robert Louis Stevenson*

The best way to keep your friends is not to give them away.
*Wilson Mizner*

Give me the avowed, the erect, the manly foe,
Bold I can meet—perhaps may turn his blow;
But of all plagues, good Heaven, thy wrath can send,
Save, save, oh save me from the Candid Friend.
*George Canning*

## FRIENDSHIP

A true friend walks in when the rest of the world walks out.

A friend is always happy about your success—if it doesn't surpass his own.

Be slow to fall into friendship, but when thou art in continue firm and constant.
*Socrates*

Life is to be fortified by many friendships. To love, and to be loved, is the greatest happiness of existence.
*Sydney Smith*

If we were all given by magic the power to read each other's thoughts, I suppose the first effect would be to dissolve all friendships.
*Bertrand Russell*

It's important to our friends to believe that we are unreservedly frank with them, and important to friendship that we are not.
*Mignon McLaughlin*

Friendship is like a bank account. You can't continue to draw on it without making deposits.

Friendship is a sheltering tree.

Keep your friendships in repair.
*Ralph Waldo Emerson*

Just as yellow gold is tested in the fire, so is friendship to be tested by adversity.
*Ovid*

Be courteous to all, but intimate with few, and let those few be well tried before you give them your confidence. True friendship is a plant of low growth, and must undergo and withstand the shocks of adversity before it is entitled to the appellation.
*George Washington*

Friendship may, and often does, grow into love, but love never subsides into friendship.
*Lord Byron*

Love is blind; friendship closes its eyes.
*Anonymous*

## FUNERALS

I did not attend his funeral; but I wrote a nice letter saying I approved of it.
*Mark Twain*

The only reason I might go to the funeral is to make absolutely sure that he's dead.
*Anthony Sampson*

## FURNITURE

Our furniture goes back to Louis XIV unless we pay Louis before the 14th.

By the time we have all the furniture paid for we'll have genuine antiques.

## FUTILITY

There is no getting blood out of a turnip.
*Italian proverb*

## FUTURE

I never think of the future. It comes soon enough.
*Albert Einstein*

Light tomorrow with today!
*Elizabeth B. Browning*

You can only predict things after they've happened.
*Eugene Ionesco*

Tomorrow is the most important thing in life. Comes into us at midnight very clean. It's perfect when it arrives and it puts itself in our hands. It hopes we've learned something from yesterday.
*John Wayne*

The trouble with our times is that the future is not what it used to be.
*Paul Valery*

The future can be anything we want it to be, providing we have the faith and that we realize that peace, no less than war, required blood and sweat and tears.

*Charles F. Kettering*

# G

GAIN—GUILT

## GAIN

No pain, no gain.

## GENIUS

Genius is only great patience.
*Count de Buffon*

When a true genius appears in the world you may know him
by this sign, that the dunces are all in confederacy against him.
*Jonathan Swift*

Everyone is a genius at least once a year; a real genius has his
original ideas closer together.
*G. C. Lichtenberg*

Genius is one percent inspiration and ninety-nine percent
perspiration.
*Thomas Edison*

Genius is nothing but labor and diligence.

Hunger is the handmaid of genius.

Adversity reveals genius, prosperity hides it.
*Horace*

Every man of genius is considerably helped by being dead.
*Robert Lynd*

## GENTLEMEN

A gentleman is a man who can disagree without being
disagreeable.

The gentleman is a Christian product.
*George H. Calvert*

This is the final test of a gentleman: his respect for those who
can be of no possible value to him.
*William Lyon Phelps*

Once a gentleman, always a gentleman.
*Charles Dickens*

He is every other inch a gentleman.
*Rebecca West*

Propriety of manners and consideration for others are the two main characteristics of a gentleman.
*Benjamin Disraeli*

. . . one who never hurts anyone's feelings intentionally.
*Oliver Herford*

## GIFTS

A gift blindeth the eyes.

He doubles his gift who gives in time.

Look not a gift horse in the mouth.

A small gift is better than a great promise.
*German proverb*

A gift, though small, is welcome.
*Greek proverb*

## GIVING

It is more blessed to give than to receive.
*Acts 20:35*

He gives double who gives unasked.
*Arabian proverb*

Give to the poor, and thou shalt have treasure in heaven.
*Matthew 19:21*

The wise man does not lay up treasure. The more he gives the more he has.
*Chinese proverb*

## GLORY

The glory of great men should be measured by the means they have used to acquire it.
*La Rochefoucauld*

When glory comes, memory departs.
*French proverb*

## GLUTTONY

His eye is bigger than his belly.

The mouth has a little hole, but it can swallow house and roof.
*Yiddish proverb*

## GOALS

It is a mistake to look too far ahead. Only one link in the chain of destiny can be handled at a time.
*Winston Churchill*

This one thing I do, forgetting those things which are behind, and reaching forth unto those things which are before, I press toward the mark.
*Philippians 3:13-14*

Arriving at one goal is the starting point to another.
*John Dewey*

## GOD

Fear that man who fears not God.

I could prove God statistically.
*George Gallup*

I can't believe that God plays dice with the universe.
*Albert Einstein*

God does not pay weekly, but he pays at the end.
*Dutch proverb*

God is our refuge and strength, a very present help in trouble.
*Psalm 46:1*

Thou shalt love the Lord thy God with all thy heart, and with all thy soul, and with all thy mind.
*Matthew 22:37*

I am the way, the truth, and the life: no man cometh unto the Father, but by me.
*John 14:6*

Fear God, and keep his commandments.
*Ecclesiastes 12:13*

Here I stand. I can do not otherwise. God help me. Amen.
*Martin Luther*

If God be for us, who can be against us?
*Romans 8:31*

God is a sure paymaster.

God moves in a mysterious way His wonders to perform.
*William Cowper*

God postpones, he does not overlook.
*Turkish proverb*

God is a father; luck, a stepfather.
*Yiddish proverb*

## GOLD
Gold is the devil's fishhook.

Kill not the goose that lays the golden eggs.

## GOLDEN RULE
Whatsoever ye would that men should do to you, do ye even so to them.
*Matthew 7:12*

## GOLF
My golf is improving. Yesterday I hit the ball in one.

A handicapped golfer is a man who plays with his boss.

In golf, the ball always lies poorly; and the player well.

Golf is the most popular way of beating around the bush.

Golf has made more liars out of the American people than the income tax.

If you watch a game, it's fun. If you play it, it's recreation. If you work at it, it's golf.
*Bob Hope*

Golf is a good walk spoiled.
*Mark Twain*

## GOOD
One good turn asketh another.

How beautiful upon the mountains are the feet of him that
bringeth good tidings, that publisheth peace.
*Isaiah 52:7*

A good life is a main argument.
*Ben Jonson*

## GOOD MANNERS

Cultivate good manners, and you'll be mistaken for a
doorman.

The test of good manners is to be able to put up pleasantly
with bad ones.

We expect our children to learn good table manners without
ever seeing any.

## GOODNESS

When you give to the poor, do not let your left hand know
what your right hand is doing.
*Matthew 6:3 (NASB)*

If a friend is in trouble, don't annoy him by asking if there is
anything you can do. Think up something appropriate and
do it.
*E. W. Howe*

Let us not be weary in well doing.
*Galatians 6:9*

If you wish to be good, first believe that you are bad.
*Greek proverb*

To a good man nothing that happens is evil.
*Greek proverb*

## GOSSIP

A gossip always gets caught in their own mouth-trap.

A gossip is a newscaster without the sponsor.

A gossip tells things before you have a chance to tell them.

She doesn't like to repeat gossip, but what else can you do
with it?

I will never repeat gossip, so please listen carefully the first time.

The difference between gossip and news is whether you hear it or tell it.

Gossip is like a grapefruit. In order to be really good, it has to be juicy.

A gossip is a person who suffers from acute indiscretion.

A closed mouth gathers no foot.

Half the evil in the world is gossip started by good people.

No gossip ever dies away entirely, if many people voice it: it, too, is a king of divinity.
*Hesiod*

Gossips and lying go together.

Whoever gossips to you will gossip of you.
*Spanish proverb*

Show me someone who never gossips, and I'll show you someone who isn't interested in people.
*Barbara Walters*

Tattlers also and busybodies, speaking things which they ought not.
*1 Timothy 5:13*

Of every ten persons who talk about you, nine will say something bad, and the tenth will say something good in a bad way.
*Antoine Rivarol*

Gossip is the art of saying nothing in a way that leaves practically nothing unsaid.
*Walter Winchell*

## GOVERNMENT

A house divided against itself cannot stand—I believe this government cannot endure permanently half-slave and half-free.
*Abraham Lincoln*

The impersonal hand of government can never replace the helping hand of a neighbor.
*Hubert Humphrey*

No government can be long secure without a formidable opposition.
*Benjamin Disraeli*

Govern yourself and you can govern the world.
*Chinese proverb*

The whole of government consists in the art of being honest.
*Thomas Jefferson*

## GOVERNMENT DEBT

When you think of the government debt the next generation must pay off, it's no wonder a baby yells when it's born.

## GRADUAL

Feather by feather the goose is plucked.

## GRAFFITI

You know you're in a tough neighborhood when you go into a confessional and there's graffiti on the walls.

There was so much handwriting on the wall that even the wall fell down.
*Christopher Morley*

## GRASS

The grass is greener on the other side of the fence.

## GRATITUDE

The gratitude of most men is but a secret desire of receiving greater benefits.
*La Rochefoucauld*

A thankful heart is the parent of all virtues.
*Cicero*

In every thing give thanks.
*1 Thessalonians 5:18*

Gratitude is the heart's memory.
*French proverb*

Nothing tires a man more than to be grateful all the time.
*E. W. Howe*

## GREATNESS

Mountains appear more lofty, the nearer they are approached, but great men resemble them not in this particular.
*Lady Blessington*

In great affairs men show themselves as they wish to be seen; in small things they show themselves as they are.
*S. Chamfort*

There's a pinch of the madman in every great man.
*French proverb*

It is unavoidable that if we learn more about a great man's life, we shall also hear of occasions on which he has done no better than we, and has in fact come nearer to us as a human being.
*Sigmund Freud*

The first virtue of all really great men is that they are sincere.
*Anatole France*

The great man is he who has not lost the heart of a child.
*Mencius*

The great man is the man who does a thing for the first time.
*Alexander Smith*

We are both great men, but I have succeeded better in keeping it a profound secret than he has.
*Bill Nye*

The greatest thought is God.
The greatest thing is love.
The greatest mystery is death.
The greatest challenge is life.
The greatest waste of time is hate and the most expensive indulgence is pride.
*Charles E. Jones*

No great thing is created suddenly.
*Epictetus*

Great and good are seldom the same man.
*Thomas Fuller*

The man who is anybody and who does anything is surely
going to be criticized, vilified, and misunderstood. This is part
of the penalty for greatness, and every man understands, too,
that it is no proof of greatness.
*Elbert Hubbard*

Lack of something to feel important about is almost the greatest tragedy a man may have.
*Arthur E. Morgan*

The secret of true greatness is simplicity.

The biggest dog has been a pup.
*Joaquin Miller*

## GREED

It is difficult to save money when your neighbors keep buying
things you can't afford.

You can't sell the cow and have the milk too.

He that serves God for money will serve the devil for more of
the same.

## GRIEF

Grief is itself a medicine.
*William Cowper*

The only cure for grief is action.
*George Henry Lewes*

Everyone can master a grief but he that has it.
*William Shakespeare*

Grief once told brings somewhat back of peace.
*W. Morris*

Great souls suffer in silence.
*F. von Schiller*

Light griefs can speak; but deeper ones are dumb.
*Latin proverb*

There is no grief which time does not lessen.
*Latin proverb*

Do not rejoice at my grief, for when mine is old, yours will be new.
*Spanish proverb*

He that conceals his grief finds no remedy for it.
*Turkish proverb*

There is no grief like the grief that does not speak.
*Henry W. Longfellow*

## GROWTH

The mother eagle teaches her little ones to fly by making their nest so uncomfortable that they are forced to leave it and commit themselves to the unknown world of air outside. And just so does our God to us. He stirs up our comfortable nests, and pushes us over the edge of them, and we are forced to use our wings to save ourselves from fatal falling. Read your trials in this light, and see if you cannot begin to get a glimpse of their meaning. Your wings are being developed.
*Hannah Whitall Smith*

There is no growth except in the fulfillment of obligations.
*Anonymous*

To be a giant and not a dwarf in your profession, you must always be growing.
*William Mathews*

There is no fruit which is not bitter before it is ripe.
*Publilius Syrus*

## GUEST

A constant guest is never welcome.

An unbidden guest knows not where to sit.

Fresh fish and new-come guests smell in three days.

Welcome the coming, speed the parting guest.

## GUILT

Let wickedness escape as it may at the bar, it never fails of doing justice upon itself; for every guilty person is his own hangman.
*Seneca*

He who flees from trial confesses his guilt.
*Publilius Syrus*

The wicked flee when no man pursueth.
*Proverbs 28:1*

Guilt is always jealous.

# H

HABIT—HYPOCRISY

# HABIT

Habit, if not resisted, soon becomes necessity.
*St. Augustine*

One of the advantages of being disorderly is that one is constantly making exciting discoveries.
*A. A. Milne*

It seems, in fact, as though the second half of a man's life is made up of nothing but the habits he has accumulated during the first half.
*Fyodor Dostoevsky*

The chains of habit are too weak to be felt until they are too strong to be broken.
*Samuel Johnson*

The nature of men is always the same; it is their habits that separate them.
*Confucius*

Habits are first cobwebs, then cables.

Nothing so needs reforming as other people's habits.
*Mark Twain*

'Tis easier to prevent bad habits than to break them.

A nail is driven out by another nail; habit is overcome by habit.
*Latin proverb*

Habit is a habit and not to be flung out of the window by any man but coaxed downstairs a step at a time.
*Mark Twain*

Good habits result from resisting temptation.
*Ancient proverb*

# HAIR

Ever since I put grease on my hair, everything slips my mind.

Gray hair is a sign of age, not of wisdom.
*Greek proverb*

## HAPPINESS

Happiness is the only thing that multiplies by division.

A poor man can be happy; but a happy man isn't poor.

Show me an optimist, and I'll show you a happy-condriac.

The happiest people are those who are too busy to notice.

Happiness is a form of courage.

Happiness has to be cranked up; trouble is a self-starter.

Happiness lies, first of all, in health.
*George William Curtis*

He that has no one to love or confide in, has little to hope.
He wants the radical principle of happiness.
*Samuel Johnson*

We have no more right to consume happiness without producing it than to consume wealth without producing it.
*George Bernard Shaw*

When one door of happiness closes, another opens; but often we look so long at the closed door that we do not see the one which has been opened for us.
*Helen Keller*

A man should always consider how much he has more than he wants, and how much more unhappy he might be than he really is.
*Joseph Addison*

If a man has important work, and enough leisure and income to enable him to do it properly, he is in possession of as much happiness as is good for any of the children of Adam.
*R. H. Tawney*

Existence is a strange bargain. Life owes us little; we owe it everything. The only true happiness comes from squandering ourselves for a purpose.
*William Cowper*

Even if we can't be happy, we must always be cheerful.
*Irving Kristol*

We act as though comfort and luxury were the chief require-
ments of life, when all that we need to make us really happy is
something to be enthusiastic about.
*Charles Kingsley*

One thing I know: The only ones among you who will be
really happy are those who will have sought and found how
to serve.
*Albert Schweitzer*

Behold, we count them happy which endure. Ye have heard of
the patience of Job.
*James 5:11*

There is only one way to happiness and that is to cease worrying about things which are beyond the power of our will.
*Epictetus*

Happiness comes fleetingly now and then,
To those who have learned to do without it,
And to them only.
*Don Marquis*

To be happy, we must not be too concerned with others.
*Albert Camus*

There is no happiness except in the realization that we have
accomplished something.
*Henry Ford Sr.*

Happiness is a habit to be cultivated.

Happiness is a way-station between too little and too much.

'Tis not good to be happy too young.

One is never as happy or as unhappy as he thinks.
*La Rochefoucauld*

The happiest people seem to be those who have no particular
reason for being happy except that they are so.
*W. R. Inge*

One day's happiness makes a man forget his misfortune; and
one day's misfortune makes him forget his past happiness.
*Ecclesiasticus*

Ask yourself whether you are happy, and you cease to be so.
*John Stuart Mill*

Grief can take care of itself, but to get the full value from joy you must have somebody to divide it with.
*Mark Twain*

It is pretty hard to tell what does bring happiness; poverty and wealth have both failed.
*Kin Hubbard*

Be happy while you're living, for you're a long time dead.
*Scottish proverb*

The grand essentials of happiness are: something to do, something to love, and something to hope for.
*Allan K. Chalmers*

## HARVEST
He that observeth the wind shall not sow; and he that regardeth the clouds shall not reap.
*Ecclesiastes 11:4*

## HASTE
Do in haste and repent at leisure.

Haste makes waste.

Haste manages all things badly.
*Latin proverb*

Who pours water hastily into a bottle spills more than goes in.
*Spanish proverb*

## HATRED
Hatred watches while friendship sleeps.
*French proverb*

Hatred stirreth up strifes: but love covereth all sins.
*Proverbs 10:12*

Hate and mistrust are the children of blindness.

Hate knows no age but death.

Hating people is like burning down your own house to get rid of a rat.
*H. E. Fosdick*

Hatred is self-punishment.

Hatred is the coward's revenge for being intimidated.
*George Bernard Shaw*

He who is hated by all cannot expect to live long.
*French proverb*

Hatred is a settled anger.
*Latin proverb*

We hate whom we have injured.
*Latin proverb*

Whom men fear they hate, and whom they hate they wish dead.
*Latin proverb*

To hate fatigues.
*Jean Rostand*

Hatred comes from the heart; contempt from the head; and neither feeling is quite within our control.
*Arthur Schopenhauer*

## HEAD

One way to get ahead and stay ahead is to use your head.

No man's head aches while he comforts another.

He that has a head of glass must not throw stones at another.
*Italian proverb*

When the head aches, all the body is out of tune.
*Spanish proverb*

A big head has a big ache.
*Turkish proverb*

## HEALTH

He who has health has hope, and he who has hope has everything.
*Arabian proverb*

Health is the thing that makes you feel that now is the best time of the year.
*Franklin Pierce Adams*

The greatest mistake a man can make is to sacrifice health for any other advantage.
*Arthur Schopenhauer*

A good wife and health is man's best wealth.

The best doctors in the world are Doctor Diet, Doctor Quiet, and Doctor Merryman.

Before supper walk a little, after supper do the same.
*Latin proverb*

Good health and good sense are two great blessings.
*Latin proverb*

## HEALTH FOOD
Health food makes me sick.
*Calvin Trillin*

## HEART
Where your treasure is, there will your heart be also.
*Matthew 6:21*

A merry heart maketh a cheerful countenance.
*Proverbs 15:13*

He that is of a merry heart hath a continual feast.
*Proverbs 15:15*

Out of the abundance of the heart the mouth speaketh.
*Matthew 12:34*

The heart is deceitful above all things, and desperately wicked.
*Jeremiah 17:9*

Every heart hath its own ache.

The selfish heart deserves the pain it feels.

A happy heart is better than a full purse.
*Italian proverb*

The heart's testimony is stronger than a thousand witnesses.
*Turkish proverb*

## HEARTY MEAL

Don't ever go into water after a hearty meal. You'll never find it there.

## HELL

The safest road to Hell is the gradual one—the gentle slope, soft underfoot, without sudden turnings, without milestones, without signposts.
*C. S. Lewis*

Hell is truth seen too late.
*Anonymous*

The road to Hell is paved with good intentions.

Hell hath no fury like a woman scorned.

## HERO

Being a hero is about the shortest-lived profession on earth.
*Will Rogers*

When the heroes go off the stage, the clowns come on.
*Heinrich Heine*

I am convinced that a light supper, a good night's sleep, and a fine morning, have sometimes made a hero of the same man, who, by indigestion, a restless night, and rainy morning, would have proved a coward.
*Lord Chesterfield*

The really great man is the man who makes every man feel great.
*G. K. Chesterton*

The main thing about being a hero is to know when to die.
*Will Rogers*

## HIGH POINT

The other night, while lying on the couch, I reviewed the high point of my life and fell asleep.

## HIRING

The best time to fire a person is before you hire them.
*R. E. Phillips*

Hiring is a manager's most important job.
*Peter F. Drucker*

## HISTORY

Most history is a record of the triumphs, disasters and follies of top people. The black hole in it is the way of life of mute, inglorious men and women who made no nuisance of themselves in the world.
*Philip Howard*

History never looks like history when you are living through it. It always looks confusing and messy, and it always feels uncomfortable.
*John W. Gardner*

Don't brood on what's past, but never forget it either.
*Thomas H. Raddall*

More history is made by secret handshakes than by battles, bills and proclamations.
*John Barth*

We should keep the Panama Canal. After all we stole it fair and square.
*S. I. Hayakawa*

History repeats itself.

## HOME

A man travels the world over in search of what he needs and returns home to find it.
*George Moore*

Be it ever so humble, there's no place like home.
*J. H. Payne*

A comfortable house is a great source of happiness. It ranks immediately after health and a good conscience.
*Sydney Smith*

A hundred men may make an encampment, but it takes a woman to make a home.
*Chinese proverb*

## HOMO SAPIENS

The strongest human instinct is to impart information, the second strongest is to resist it.
*Kenneth Graham*

Who is wise? He that learns from everyone.
Who is powerful? He that governs his passions.
Who is rich? He that is content.
Who is that? Nobody.
*Benjamin Franklin*

## HONESTY

Honesty is the best policy, but there are too few policyholders.

No legacy is so rich as honesty.
*William Shakespeare*

Everybody has a little bit of Watergate in him.
*Billy Graham*

Anger cannot be dishonest.
*George R. Bach*

An honest man's the noblest work of God.
*Alexander Pope*

Honesty is a fine jewel, but much out of fashion.

## HONOR

Honour thy father and thy mother.
*Exodus 20:12*

Who loses honor can lose nothing else.
*Latin proverb*

It is better to deserve honors and not have them than to have them and not deserve them.
*Mark Twain*

Better to die ten thousand deaths than wound my honor.
*Joseph Addison*

Dignity does not consist in possessing honours, but in deserving them.
*Aristotle*

No revenge is more honorable than the one not taken.
*Spanish proverb*

## HOPE

To the sick, while there is life there is hope.
*Cicero*

Hope deferred makes the heart sick.
*Proverbs 13:12 (NIV)*

Every thing that is done in the world is done by hope.
*Martin Luther*

## HOSPITAL

I know that hospital costs are out of hand—but I never thought I'd see a self-service operating table.

## HOSPITALITY

Be not forgetful to entertain strangers: for thereby some have entertained angels unawares.
*Hebrews 13:2*

## HOT WATER

The best way to keep your daughter out of hot water is to put some dishes in it.

## HUMAN COMEDY

Of all days, the day on which one has not laughed is surely the most wasted.
*S. Chamfort*

It is not enough to possess wit. One must have enough of it to avoid having too much.
*André Maurois*

## HUMAN NATURE

The best time to study human nature is when you are alone.

## HUMAN RELATIONS

A sense of duty is useful in work, but offensive in personal relations. People wish to be liked, not be endured with patient resignation.
*Bertrand Russell*

We wander through this life together in a semi-darkness in which none of us can distinguish exactly the features of his neighbour. Only from time to time, through some experience that we have of our companion, or through some remark that he passes, he stands for a moment close to us, as though illuminated by a flash of lightning. Then we see him as he really is.
*Albert Schweitzer*

A hundred times every day I remind myself that my inner and outer life depend on the labours of other men, living and dead, and that I must exert myself in order to give in the same measure as I have received.
*Albert Einstein*

## HUMILITY

I believe the first test of a truly great man is his humility.
*John Ruskin*

## HUMOR

Humor is like history, it repeats itself.

Everybody likes a kidder, but nobody lends him money.
*Arthur Miller*

Good humor makes all things tolerable.
*Henry Ward Beecher*

Everything is funny as long as it happens to somebody else.

Humor is gravity concealed behind a jest.

If I studied all my life, I couldn't think up half the number of funny things passed in one session of Congress.
*Will Rogers*

The satirist shoots to kill while the humorist brings his prey back alive and eventually releases him again for another chance.
*Peter de Vries*

Humour can be dissected, as a frog can, but the thing dies in the process.
*E. B. White*

The love of truth lies at the root of much humor.

## HUNGER

A hungry man is an angry man.

## HUSBAND

As the husband is, the wife is.
*Alfred, Lord Tennyson*

The husband who wants a happy marriage should learn to keep his mouth shut and his checkbook open.
*Groucho Marx*

## HYPOCHONDRIAC

A hypochondriac can't leave being well-enough alone.

One illness you can catch from a hypochondriac is a pain in the neck.

A frustrated hypochondriac is one who is allergic to medicine.

My neighbor is such a hypochondriac that he filled his water bed with chicken soup.

The trouble with being a hypochondriac these days is that antibiotics have cured all the good diseases.
*Caskie Stinnet*

## HYPOCRISY

Saint abroad, and a devil at home.
*John Bunyan*

When the fox preaches, look to your geese.
*German proverb*

For an idea ever to be fashionable is ominous, since it must afterwards be always old-fashioned.
*George Santayana*

IDEAS—IRS

## IDEAS

To some people a bright idea is beginner's luck.

The best ideas are common property.
*Seneca*

If you want to get across an idea, wrap it up in a person.
*Ralph Bunche*

Nothing is more dangerous than an idea, when a man has only one idea.
*Alain*

It is only liquid currents of thought that move men and the world.
*Wendell Phillips*

I am more of a sponge than an inventor. I absorb ideas from every source. My principal business is giving commercial value to the brilliant but misdirected ideas of others.
*Thomas Edison*

I could not sleep when I got on a hunt for an idea, until I had caught it; and when I thought I had got it, I was not satisfied until I had repeated it over and over again, until I had put it in language plain enough as I thought, for any boy I knew to comprehend.
*Abraham Lincoln*

## IDENTITY

The voice is a second face.
*Gerard Bauer*

People often say that this or that person has not yet found himself. But the self is not something one finds, it is something one creates.
*Thomas Szasz*

Whatever you may be sure of, be sure of this: that you are dreadfully like other people.
*James Russell Lowell*

## IDLENESS

Some people have a perfect genius for doing nothing, and doing it assiduously.
*Thomas Haliburton*

It is impossible to enjoy idling thoroughly, unless one has plenty of work to do.
*Jerome K. Jerome*

With enough "ifs" we could put Paris into a bottle.
*French proverb*

An idle brain is the devil's shop.

Expect poison from the standing water.
*William Blake*

Idleness is the root of all mischief.

Laziness travels so slowly that poverty soon overtakes him.

To do nothing is in every man's power.
*Samuel Johnson*

It is only idle people who can find time for everything.
*French proverb*

Idleness has poverty for wages.
*German proverb*

Idleness is ever the root of indecision.
*Latin proverb*

They do nothing laboriously.
*Latin proverb*

Laziness grows on people; it begins in cobwebs and ends in iron chains.
*Thomas Fowell Buxton*

## IGNORANCE

Ignorance is the necessary condition of life itself. If we knew everything, we could not endure existence for a single hour.
*Anatole France*

Being ignorant is not so much a shame as being unwilling
to learn.

Where ignorance is bliss, 'tis folly to be wise.
*Thomas Gray*

Ignorance of one's misfortunes is clear gain.
*Greek proverb*

What you don't know would make a great book.
*Sydney Smith*

He knows so little and knows it so fluently.
*Ellen Glasgow*

## ILLNESS

Illness tells us what we are.
*Italian proverb*

The sorrow which has no vent in tears may make other organs
weep.
*Henry Maudsley*

If a man thinks about his physical or moral state, he usually
discovers that he is ill.
*Johann Goethe*

I reckon being ill is one of the greatest pleasures of life,
provided one is not too ill and is not obliged to work till one
is better.
*Samuel Butler*

For the mental patient's family and society, mental illness is a
"problem"; for the patient himself it is a "solution."
*Thomas Szasz*

'Tis a good ill that comes alone.

Illness is not something a person has. It's another way of being.
*Jonathan Miller*

## IMAGINATION

Imagination makes a man think he can run the business
better than the boss.

Imagination disposes of everything; it creates beauty, justice, and happiness, which is everything in this world.
*Blaise Pascal*

Man's mind once stretched by a new idea, never regains its original dimension.
*Oliver Wendell Holmes*

Imagination is more important than knowledge.
*Albert Einstein*

## IMMORTALITY
If I have any belief about immortality, it is that certain dogs I have known will go to Heaven, and very, very few persons.
*James Thurber*

The reward of great men is that, long after they have died, one is not quite sure that they are dead.
*Jules Renard*

## IMPRESSION
You never get a second chance to make a good first impression.

## IMPROVEMENT
People seldom improve when they have no other model but themselves to copy after.
*Oliver Goldsmith*

## INCOME
Income is a small matter to me—especially after taxes.

Income is something you can't live without or within.

Income always looks bigger coming than going.

I don't live within my income because I can't afford it.

## INDECISION
No man, having put his hand to the plough, and looking back, is fit for the kingdom of God.
*Luke 9:62*

Through indecision opportunity is often lost.
*Latin proverb*

We know what happens to people who stay in the middle of
the road. They get run over.
*Aneurin Bevan*

Indecision is debilitating; it feeds upon itself; it is, one might
almost say, habit-forming. Not only that, but it is contagious;
it transmits itself to others.
*H. A. Hopf*

Don't swap horses when you are crossing a stream.
*Abraham Lincoln*

## INDEPENDENCE
I would rather sit on a pumpkin and have it all to myself than
be on a crowded velvet cushion.
*Henry David Thoreau*

## INDIFFERENCE
Once conform, once do what others do because they do it, and
a kind of lethargy steals over all the finer senses of the soul.
*Michel de Montaigne*

## INDIVIDUALITY
Dare to be what you are and to believe in your own
individuality.
*Henri Amiel*

Resolve to be thyself.
*Matthew Arnold*

In order to be irreplaceable one must always be different.
*Coco Chanel*

Things have various qualities and the soul various tendencies,
for nothing presented to the soul is simple, and the soul never
applies itself simply to any subject. That is why the same
thing makes us laugh and cry.
*Blaise Pascal*

The shoe that fits one person pinches another; there is no recipe for living that suits all cases.
*Carl Jung*

## INDUSTRY

Everything comes to him who hustles while he waits.
*Thomas Edison*

Elbow grease gives the best polish.

Like the bee, we should make our industry our amusement.
*Oliver Goldsmith*

A man who gives his children habits of industry provides for them better than by giving them a fortune.
*Richard Whately*

In the ordinary business of life, industry can do anything which genius can do, and very many things which it cannot.
*Henry Ward Beecher*

## INFERIORITY

No man likes to have his intelligence or good faith questioned, especially if he has doubts about it himself.
*Henry Brooks Adams*

We must interpret a bad temper as a sign of inferiority.
*Alfred Adler*

No two men can be half an hour together but one shall acquire an evident superiority over the other.
*Samuel Johnson*

## INFLATION

Two can live as cheaply as one, and they generally have to.

Inflation is a shot in the arm that leaves a pain in the neck.

Inflation is when you eat three square meals a day and pay for six.

Never have so many people lived so well, so far behind, before.

Inflation is when you have to make twice as much money to keep up with your standard of living of last year—when you declared bankruptcy.

## INFLUENCE

Let him that would move the world, first move himself.
*Socrates*

## INFORMATION

Foolish are the generals who ignore the daily intelligence from the trenches.
*Anonymous*

## INGRATITUDE

How sharper than a serpent's tooth it is to have a thankless child!
*William Shakespeare*

Ingratitude is the mother of every vice.
*French proverb*

Ingratitude is the daughter of pride.
*Spanish proverb*

## INITIATIVE

If there is no wind, row.
*Latin proverb*

Ask, and it shall be given you; seek, and ye shall find; knock, and it shall be opened unto you.
*Matthew 7:7*

He who seizes the right moment is the right man.
*Johann Goethe*

The first blow is half the battle.
*Oliver Goldsmith*

Fortune sides with him who dares.
*Virgil*

Initiative consists of doing the right thing without being told.
*Irving Mack*

## INJURY

The injury we do and the one we suffer are not weighted in the same scales.
*Aesop*

It costs more to revenge injuries than to bear them.

The remedy for injuries is to forget them.
*Latin proverb*

No man is hurt but by himself.
*Diogenes*

Never does the human soul appear so strong as when it foregoes revenge and dares to forgive an injury.
*Edwin Hubbel Chapin*

## INJUSTICE

He who commits injustice is ever made more wretched than he who suffers it.
*Plato*

If thou suffer injustice, console thyself; the true unhappiness is in doing it.
*Democritus*

Those who commit injustice bear the greatest burden.
*Hosea Ballou*

## INNOCENCE

Whoever blushes is already guilty; true innocence is ashamed of nothing.
*Jean-Jacques Rousseau*

Innocence is its own defense.

## INNOVATION

Even when I was young I suspected that much might be done in a better way.
*Henry Ford Sr.*

## INQUISITIVE

He who peeps through a hole may see what will vex him.

He that pries into every cloud may be stricken with a thunderbolt.

## INSANITY

When we remember we are all mad, the mysteries disappear and life stands explained.
*Mark Twain*

## INSOLENCE

Insolence is pride with her mask pulled off.

## INSTINCT

Trust the instinct to the end, though you can render no reason.
*Ralph Waldo Emerson*

## INSULT

It is often better not to see an insult than to avenge it.
*Seneca*

An injury is much sooner forgiven than an insult.

If you speak insults, you shall also hear them.
*Latin proverb*

The best way to procure insults is to submit them.
*William Hazlitt*

There are two insults no human being will endure: that he has no sense of humor, and that he has never known trouble.
*Sinclair Lewis*

A graceful taunt is worth a thousand insults.
*Louis Nizer*

A fly, Sir, may sting a stately horse and make him wince; but one is but an insect, and the other a horse still.
*Samuel Johnson*

Woe unto you, when all men shall speak well of you!
*Luke 6:26*

He that flings dirt at another dirtieth himself most.
*Thomas Fuller*

It takes your enemy and your friend, working together, to hurt you to the heart; the one to slander you and the other to get the news to you.
*Mark Twain*

Abuse a man unjustly, and you will make friends for him.
*Howe*

If I have said something to hurt a man once, I shall not get the better of this by saying many things to please him.
*Samuel Johnson*

## INSURANCE

In every insurance policy the big print giveth and the small print taketh away.

I thought my group insurance plan was fine until I found out I couldn't collect unless the whole group is sick.

## INTELLIGENCE

Intelligence is quickness in seeing things as they are.
*George Santayana*

An intelligent person often talks with his eyes; a shallow man often swallows with his ears.
*Mr. Tut-Tut*

The test of a first-rate intelligence is the ability to hold two opposed ideas at the same time, and still retain the ability to function.
*F. Scott Fitzgerald*

## INTROVERT

At least an introvert spends his time minding his own business.

## INTUITION

Follow your hunches like the ancient navigators followed the stars. The voyage may be lonely, but the stars will take you where you want to go.
*David J. Mahoney*

Intuition is reason in a hurry.
*Holbrook Jackson*

Intuition will tell the thinking mind where to look next.
*Jonas Salk*

## INVENTION

Great discoveries and improvements invariably involve the cooperation of many minds. I may be given credit for having blazed the trail but when I look at the subsequent developments I feel the credit is due to others rather than to myself.
*Alexander Graham Bell*

## INVESTMENT

The best investment is in the tools of one's own trade.
*Benjamin Franklin*

Live on half of what you make and invest the rest in land.
*Will Rogers*

## IRS

One thing that keeps a man from holding his own is the IRS.

J

JEALOUSY—JUSTICE

## JEALOUSY

Jealousy is nourished by doubt.
*French proverb*

To jealousy, nothing is more frightful than laughter.
*Françoise Sagan*

A jealous man always finds more than he is looking for.
*Madeleine de Scudéry*

There is never jealousy where there is not strong regard.
*Washington Irving*

Lots of people know a good thing the minute the other fellow sees it first.
*Job E. Hedges*

## JEST

The worst jests are those which are true.
*French proverb*

The jesting of wits, like the playing of puppies, often ends in snarling.

A jest is half a truth.
*Yiddish proverb*

Said in sport, meant in earnest.
*German proverb*

## JESUS CHRIST

If you [General Bertrand] do not perceive that Jesus Christ is God, very well: then I did wrong to make you a general.
*Napoleon Bonaparte*

## JOKE

A joke never gains over an enemy, but often loses a friend.

The man who doesn't laugh at a funny joke is probably not employed by the man who told it.

The man who says his wife can't take a joke forgets himself.

A bad joke is like a bad egg—all the worse for having been cracked.

## JOURNALIST

A journalist is a grumbler, a censurer, a giver of advice, a regent of sovereigns, a tutor of nations. Four hostile newspapers are more to be feared than a thousand bayonets.
*Napoleon Bonaparte*

## JOY

A joy that's shared is a joy made double.

One can endure sorrow alone, but it takes two to be glad.
*Elbert Hubbard*

## JUDGE

He who is a judge between two friends loses one of them.
*French proverb*

## JUDGMENT

Many complain of their memory, but few of their judgment.

I mistrust the judgment of every man in a case in which his own wishes are concerned.
*First Duke of Wellington*

At the day of judgment we shall not be asked what we have read but what we have done.
*Thomas à Kempis*

## JUSTICE

Delay of justice is injustice.
*Walter S. Landor*

He who decides a case without hearing the other side, though he decide justly, cannot be considered just.
*Seneca*

If all men were just, there would be no need of valor.
*Greek proverb*

Children are innocent and love justice, while most adults are wicked and prefer mercy.
*G. K. Chesterton*

One man's word is no man's word; we should quietly hear both sides.
*Johann Goethe*

# K

KINDNESS—KNOWLEDGE

## KINDNESS

I expect to pass through life but once. If, therefore, there be any kindness I can show, or any good thing I can do to any fellow being, let me do it now, for I shall not pass this way again.
*William Penn*

Real generosity is doing something nice for someone who'll never find it out.
*Frank A. Clark*

Kindness consists in loving people more than they deserve.
*Joseph Joubert*

Human kindness has never weakened the stamina or softened the fiber of a free people. A nation does not have to be cruel in order to be tough.
*Franklin D. Roosevelt*

Kindness is a language the dumb can speak and the deaf can hear and understand.
*Christian Nestel Bovee*

You cannot do a kindness too soon, for you never know how soon it will be too late.
*Ralph Waldo Emerson*

## KISS

Stealing a kiss may be petty larceny, but usually it's grand.

A peculiar proposition. Of no use to one, yet absolute bliss to two. The small boy gets it for nothing, the young man has to lie for it, and the old man has to buy it. The baby's right, the lover's privilege, and the hypocrite's mask. To a young girl, faith; to a married woman, hope; and to an old maid, charity.
*V. P. I. Skipper*

It is the passion that is in a kiss that gives to it its sweetness; it is the affection in a kiss that sanctifies it.
*Christian Nestell Bovee*

## KNOWLEDGE

The person who knows everything has the most to learn.

Nothing annoys me more than a man who thinks he knows it all and does.

Strange how much you've got to know before you know how little you know.

To be conscious that you are ignorant is a great step to knowledge.
*Benjamin Disraeli*

One cannot know everything.
*Horace*

He who has knowledge spares his words.
*Proverbs 17:27 (NKJV)*

As we acquire more knowledge, things do not become more comprehensible, but more mysterious.
*Albert Schweitzer*

I do not pretend to know what many ignorant men are sure of.
*Clarence Darrow*

It is better to know nothing than to know what ain't so.
*Josh Billings*

He that increaseth knowledge increaseth sorrow.
*Ecclesiastes 1:18*

A little knowledge is a dangerous thing.
*Alexander Pope*

He that knows little often repeats it.

Knowledge is power.

What a man knows is everywhere at war with what he wants.
*Joseph Wood Krutch*

L

LABELS—LYING

## LABELS

Don't rely too much on labels,
For too often they are fables.
*Charles H. Spurgeon*

## LABOR

Labor disgraces no man; unfortunately you occasionally find
men disgrace labor.
*Ulysses S. Grant*

Man is so made that he can only find relaxation from one
kind of labour by taking up another.
*Anatole France*

A man is not idle because he is absorbed in thought. There is
a visible labor and there is an invisible labor.
*Victor Hugo*

The bad workmen are decidedly of the opinion that bad
workmen ought to receive the same wages as the good.
*John Stuart Mill*

Men are made stronger on realization that the helping hand
they need is at the end of their own right arm.
*Sidney J. Phillips*

Sweet is the memory of past labor.
*Greek proverb*

He who would eat the kernel must crack the shell.
*Latin proverb*

The fruit derived from labor is the sweetest of all pleasures.
*Luc de Clapiers*

## LANGUAGE

English is a funny language. A fat chance and a slim chance
are the same thing.

In Paris they simply stared when I spoke to them in French;
I never did succeed in making those idiots understand their
own language.
*Mark Twain*

A language is a dialect that has an army and navy.
*Max Weinreich*

Before using a fine word, make a place for it!
*Joseph Joubert*

Language is the dress of thought.
*Samuel Johnson*

## LAS VEGAS
It is possible to come back from Las Vegas with a small fortune if you went there with a large one.

I sure was lucky in Las Vegas. I forgot my wallet.

## LATE
Better late than never, but better never late.

He who rises late must trot all day.
*French proverb*

It is too late to come with the water when the house is burned down.
*Italian proverb*

## LAUGHTER
He who laughs, lasts.

To provoke laughter without joining in it greatly heightens the effect.
*Honore Balzac*

Ill-timed laughter is a dangerous evil.
*Greek proverb*

All things are cause for either laughter or weeping.
*Latin proverb*

A maid that laughs is half taken.

I like the laughter that opens the lips and the heart, that shows at the same time pearls and the soul.
*Charles E. Jones*

A merry heart doeth good like a medicine.
*Proverbs 17:22*

Laughter is the sun that drives winter from the human face.
*Victor Hugo*

A good laugh is sunshine in a house.

When the mouse laughs at the cat, there's a hole nearby.
*Nigerian proverb*

He laughs best who laughs last.

He who tickles himself may laugh when he pleases.
*German proverb*

Laugh, if you are wise.
*Latin proverb*

To condemn by a cutting laugh comes readily to all.
*Latin proverb*

Laugh, and the world laughs with you; weep, and you weep alone.
*Ella Wheeler Wilcox*

What is viler than to be laughed at?
*Latin proverb*

Laughter is the closest thing to the grace of God.
*Karl Barth*

Laughter is the shortest distance between two people.
*Victor Borge*

We are all here for a spell; get all the good laughs you can.
*Will Rogers*

No one is more profoundly sad than he who laughs too much.
*Jean Paul Richter*

## LAW

Someone has tabulated that we have 35 million laws on the books to enforce the Ten Commandments.
*Bert Masterson*

Where law ends, there tyranny begins.
*William Pitt*

He that goes to law holds a wolf by the ears.

Laws are like cobwebs which catch small flies, but let wasps and hornets break through.
*Jonathan Swift*

Laws too gentle are seldom obeyed; too severe, seldom executed.
*Benjamin Franklin*

If you have ten thousand regulations you destroy all respect for the law.
*Winston Churchill*

I've been told that since the beginning of civilization, millions and millions of laws have not improved on the Ten Commandments one bit.
*Ronald Reagan*

## LAWYERS

Lawyers sometimes tell the truth—they'll do anything to win a case.

My lawyer was hurt—the ambulance backed up suddenly.

Some men inherit money, some earn it, and some are lawyers.

A lawyer is a man who profits by your experience.

A poor man between two lawyers is like a fish between two cats.

As well open an oyster without a knife as a lawyer's mouth without a fee.

I know you lawyers can with ease
Twist words and meanings as you please.
*John Gay*

## LAZINESS

Laziness is often mistaken for patience.
*French proverb*

A lazy boy and a warm bed are difficult to part.
*Danish proverb*

The less I have to do, the less time I find to do it in.

# LEADER

If two men ride on a horse, one must ride behind.

When you are getting kicked from the rear it means you're in front.
*Fulton Sheen*

When you come into the presence of a leader of men, you know that you have come into the presence of fire—that it is best not uncautiously to touch that man—that there is something that makes it dangerous to cross him.
*Woodrow Wilson*

A true leader always keeps an element of surprise up his sleeve, which others cannot grasp but which keeps his public excited and breathless.
*Charles de Gaulle*

The manager administers, the leader innovates. The manager maintains, the leader develops. The manager relies on systems, the leader relies on people. The manager counts on controls, the leader counts on trust. The manager does things right, the leader does the right thing.
*Fortune magazine*

Show me a country, a company, or an organization that is doing well and I'll show you a good leader.
*Joseph E. Brooks*

It is reassuring for people to feel they have a boss, someone who knows the answers and has charted the course.
*George Cukor*

In the simplest terms, a leader is one who knows where he wants to go, gets up, and goes.
*John Erskine*

A leader is best when people barely know that he exists. When his work is done, his aim fulfilled, they will all say, "We did it ourselves."
*Lao-tzu*

A gifted leader is one who is capable of touching your heart.
*J. S. Potofsky*

Without a shepherd, sheep are not a flock.
*Russian proverb*

They that govern the most make the least noise.
*John Selden*

The outstanding leaders of every age are those who set up their own quotas and constantly exceed them.
*Thomas Watson*

He that would govern others, first should be master of himself.
*Philip Massinger*

The final test of a leader is that he leaves behind in other men the conviction and the will to carry on.
*Walter Lippmann*

## LEADERSHIP

Seven ingredients of military leadership:
He should be able to sit back and avoid getting immersed in detail.
He must not be petty.
He must not be pompous.
He should trust those under him and let them get on with their job without interference.
He must have the power of clear decision.
He should inspire confidence.

I suppose leadership at one time meant muscles; but today it means getting along with people.
*Indira Gandhi*

Anyone who critically analyzes a business learns this: that success or failure of an enterprise depends usually upon one man.
*Louis D. Brandeis*

The ability to recognize a problem before it becomes an emergency.
*Arnold H. Glasow*

Being a general calls for different talents from being a soldier.
*Titus Livy*

The inevitable end of multiple chiefs is that they fade and disappear for lack of unity.
*Napoleon Bonaparte*

A ship, to run a straight course, can have but one pilot and one steering wheel. The same applies to the successful operation of a business. There cannot be a steering wheel at every seat in an organization.
*Jules Ormont*

Keep your fears to yourself, but share your courage with others.
*Robert Louis Stevenson*

For if the trumpet give an uncertain sound, who shall prepare himself to the battle?
*1 Corinthians 14:8*

## LEAP
Look before you leap.

## LEARNING
As the old cock crows, so crows the young.

The eagle never lost so much time as when he submitted to learn from the crow.
*William Blake*

What we learn with pleasure we never forget.
*Louis Mercier*

Learning makes the wise wiser, and the fool more foolish.

Much learning shows how little mortals know.

A learned man has always wealth in himself.
*Latin proverb*

It takes ten pounds of common sense to carry one pound of learning.
*Persian proverb*

I pay the schoolmaster, but 'tis the schoolboys that educate my son.
*Ralph Waldo Emerson*

To teach is to learn twice.
*Joseph Joubert*

Experience is a good teacher, but she sends in terrific bills.
*Minna Antrim*

A learned fool is one who has read everything, and simply remembered it.
*Josh Billings*

## LEAVING
Leave off while the play is good.

## LEISURE
Leisure is the mother of philosophy.
*Thomas Hobbes*

He does not seem to me to be a free man who does not sometimes do nothing.
*Cicero*

## LEND
Lend to an enemy, and you'll gain him; to a friend, and you'll lose him.

Seldom comes a loan laughing home.

He who lends to the poor gets his interest from God.
*German proverb*

You buy yourself an enemy when you lend a man money.
*Yiddish proverb*

## LETTER
I have made this letter longer than usual because I lack the time to make it shorter.
*Blaise Pascal*

Never read over your old letters.
*G. de Maupassant*

One of the pleasures of reading old letters is the knowledge that they need no answer.
*Lord Byron*

# LIAR

A liar is not believed even though he tell the truth.
*Cicero*

Show me a liar, and I'll show you a thief.
*French proverb*

# LIBERTY

Liberty is the only thing you cannot have unless you are willing to give it to others.
*William Allen White*

When liberty destroys order, the hunger for order will destroy liberty.
*Will Durant*

These are the times that try men's souls. The summer soldier and the sunshine patriot will, in this crisis, shrink from the service of their country, but he that stands it now, deserves the love and thanks of man and woman. Tyranny, like hell, is not easily conquered; yet we have this consolation with us, that the harder the conflict, the more glorious the triumph.
*Thomas Paine*

Let every nation know, whether it wishes us well or ill, that we shall pay any price, bear any burden, meet any hardship, support any friend, oppose any foe, in order to assure the survival and the success of liberty.
*John F. Kennedy*

We who lived in concentration camps can remember the men who walked through the huts comforting others, giving away their last piece of bread. They may have been few in number, but they offer sufficient proof that everything can be taken from a man but one thing: the last of human freedoms—to choose one's attitude in any given set of circumstances—to choose one's own way.
*Viktor Frankl*

When you have robbed a man of everything, he is no longer in your power. He is free again.
*Alexander Solzhenitsyn*

We are in bondage to the law in order that we may be free.
*Cicero*

Eternal vigilance is the price of liberty.
*Wendell Phillips*

God grants liberty only to those who love it.

It is not good to have too much liberty.
*Blaise Pascal*

Liberty means responsibility. That is why most men dread it.
*George Bernard Shaw*

He that would make his own liberty secure must guard even his enemy from oppression.
*Thomas Paine*

The condition upon which God hath given liberty to man is eternal vigilance.
*John Philpot Curran*

## LIE

Ask me no questions and I'll tell you no fibs.
*Oliver Goldsmith*

Never chase a lie. Let it alone, and it will run itself to death.
I can work out a good character much faster than anyone can lie me out of it.
*Lyman Beecher*

Half the truth is often a great lie.

One of the striking differences between a cat and a lie is that a cat has only nine lives.
*Mark Twain*

Sin has many tools, but a lie is a handle which fits them all.
*Oliver Wendell Holmes*

## LIFE

I am the way, the truth, and the life: no man cometh unto the Father, but by me.
*Jesus Christ (John 14:6)*

People are living longer now; they have to—who can afford to die?

Life is now in session. Are you present?
*B. Copeland*

Life is like an onion: you peel it off one layer at a time, and sometimes you weep.
*Carl Sandburg*

Abortion is advocated only by persons who have themselves been born.
*Ronald Reagan*

Life only demands from the strength you possess. Only one feat is possible—not to have run away.
*Dag Hammarskjold*

In three words I can sum up everything I've learned about life. It goes on.
*Robert Frost*

Life is what happens to us while we are making other plans.
*Thomas la Mance*

You've got to keep fighting—you've got to risk your life every six months to stay alive.
*Elia Kazan*

You only live once—but if you work it right, once is enough.
*Joe E. Lewis*

A single event can awaken within us a stranger totally unknown to us. To live is to be slowly born.
*Antoine de Saint-Exupéry*

One man in his time plays many parts.
*William Shakespeare*

The true meaning of life is to plant trees, under whose shade you do not expect to sit.
*Nelson Henderson*

Oh, how daily life is.
*Jules Laforgue*

To live is Christ, and to die is gain.
*Philippians 1:21*

The secret of life is not to do what you like, but to like what you do.

Live and let live.
*German proverb*

Live today, forget the past.
*Greek proverb*

Live and learn.
*Italian proverb*

Live as if you were to die tomorrow.
*Latin proverb*

Our days on the earth are as a shadow.
*1 Chronicles 29:15*

Life can only be understood backwards; but it must be lived forwards.
*S. A. Kierkegaard*

He who lives a long life must pass through much evil.
*Spanish proverb*

Life is a great bundle of little things.
*Oliver Wendell Holmes Jr.*

The stone fell on the pitcher? Woe to the pitcher. The pitcher fell on the stone? Woe to the pitcher.
*Rabbinic saying*

Life consists of what a man is thinking of all day.
*Ralph Waldo Emerson*

When I hear somebody sigh that "life is hard," I am always tempted to ask, "Compared to what?"
*Sydney J. Harris*

## LIFE INSURANCE
Life insurance is what keeps a man poor all of this life so he can die rich.

## LIGHT

Hide not your light under a bushel.

## LIKE

Like pot, like cover.
*Dutch proverb*

## LIMITATIONS

One cannot manage too many affairs; like pumpkins in water, one pops up while you try to hold down the other.
*Chinese proverb*

One cannot, as the Americans say, play every instrument in the band.
*Elliot Paul*

## LION

Destroy the lion while he is yet but a whelp.

It is not good to wake a sleeping lion.

## LISTENING

A pair of good ears will drain dry a hundred tongues.

Give us grace to listen well.
*John Keble*

The only way to entertain some folks is to listen to them.
*Kin Hubbard*

It takes a great man to be a good listener.

Some people are easily entertained. All you have to do is sit down and listen to them.

A good listener is not only popular everywhere, but after a while he knows something.
*Wilson Mizner*

When you talk, you repeat what you already know; when you listen, you often learn something.
*Jaren Sparks*

## LITERATURE

It has come to be practically a sort of rule in literature that a man, having once shown himself capable of original writing, is entitled thenceforth to steal from the writings of others at discretion.
*Ralph Waldo Emerson*

## LOCK

A lock is made only for the honest man; the thief will break it.

## LONELINESS

Loneliness is and always has been the central and inevitable experience of every man.
*Thomas Wolfe*

Man's loneliness is but his fear of life.
*Eugene O'Neill*

The whole conviction of my life now rests upon the belief that loneliness, far from being a rare and curious phenomenon, peculiar to myself and to a few other solitary men, is the central and inevitable fact of human existence.
*Thomas Wolfe*

## LOOK

One must look for one thing only, to find many.
*Cesare Pavese*

## LOSING

Some people are good losers, and others can't act.

Victory has a hundred fathers but defeat is an orphan.
*Galeazzo Ciano*

Better lose the anchor than the whole ship.
*Dutch proverb*

Losers seekers, finders keepers.

Lose an hour in the morning, and you will spend all day looking for it.
*Richard Whately*

No evil is without its compensation. The less money, the less trouble; the less favor, the less envy. Even in those cases which put us out of wits, it is not the loss itself, but the estimate of the loss that troubles us.
*Seneca*

We do not know what is good until we have lost it.
*Spanish proverb*

If you've nothing to lose, you can try everything.
*Yiddish proverb*

## LOVE

Love is blind, and marriage is the eye-opener.

Love is the tie that blinds.

Love is like a game of chess. One false move and you're mated.

Scratch a lover and find a foe.
*Dorothy Parker*

Greater love hath no man than this, that a man lay down his life for his friends.
*John 15:13*

Love covers over a multitude of sins.
*1 Peter 4:8 (NIV)*

For God so loved the world, that he gave his only begotten Son, that whosoever believeth in him should not perish, but have everlasting life.
*John 3:16*

What is irritating about love is that it is a crime that requires an accomplice.
*C. Baudelaire*

Who, being loved, is poor?
*Oscar Wilde*

You will find as you look back upon your life that the moments when you have really lived are the moments when you have done things in the spirit of love.
*Henry Drummond*

The supreme happiness of life is the conviction that we are loved.
*Victor Hugo*

Love, you know, seeks to make happy rather than to be happy.
*Ralph Connor*

There is no fear in love; but perfect love casteth out fear.
*1 John 4:18*

Hatreds are the cinders of affection. It is best to be off with the old love before you go on with the new. Love is a smoke raised with the fume of sighs.
*William Shakespeare*

Love is blind, and lovers cannot see the pretty follies that themselves commit.
*William Shakespeare*

Love is like the measles—all the worse when it comes late in life.
*D. W. Jerrold*

Love maketh a wit of a fool.

Never was owl more blind than a lover.

The magic of first love is our ignorance that it can ever end.
*Benjamin Disraeli*

They do not love that do not show their love.

'Tis better to have loved and lost than never to have loved at all.
*Alfred, Lord Tennyson*

Whom we love best, to them we can say least.

Love never dies of starvation, but often of indigestion.
*French proverb*

To love is to choose.
*French proverb*

Habit causes love.
*Latin proverb*

He who says overmuch "I love not" is in love.
*Latin proverb*

Listlessness and silence denote the lover.
*Latin proverb*

Women fall in love through their ears and men through their eyes.
*Woodrow Wyatt*

A new commandment I give unto you, That ye love one another.
*Jesus Christ (John 13:34)*

Absence sharpens love, presence strengthens it.
*Thomas Fuller*

Love is a capricious creature which desires everything and can be contented with almost nothing.
*Madeleine de Scudéry*

Love makes mutes of those who habitually speak most fluently.
*Madeleine de Scudéry*

A short absence quickens love, a long absence kills it.
*Charles de Saint-Évremond*

Sudden love takes the longest time to be cured.
*Jean de La Bruyère*

It is seldom indeed that one parts on good terms, because if one were on good terms one would not part.
*Marcel Proust*

We always believe our first love is our last, and our last love our first.
*George Whyte-Melville*

## LOYALTY
Entreat me not to leave thee, or to return from following after thee: for whither thou goest, I will go; and where thou lodgest, I will lodge: thy people shall be my people, and thy God my God.
*Ruth 1:16*

## LUCK
Luck draws us for jury duty, but never for the sweepstakes.

Shallow men believe in luck. Strong men believe in cause and effect.
*Ralph Waldo Emerson*

Fortune truly helps those who are of good judgment.
*Euripides*

Luck is what happens when preparation meets opportunity.
*Elmer G. Leterman*

Depend on the rabbit's foot if you will, but remember it didn't work for the rabbit.
*R. E. Shay*

## LUXURY

Luxury is more deadly than any foe.

Luxury is the first, second and third cause of the ruin of republics. It is the vampire which soothes us into a fatal slumber while it sucks the lifeblood of our veins.
*Edward Payson*

## LYING

You can't believe some people, even when they swear they are lying.

No one can lie like a man with a secondhand car to sell.

Lying lips are an abomination to the LORD.
*Proverbs 12:22*

If we suspect that a man is lying, we should pretend to believe him for then he becomes bold and assured, lies more vigorously, and unmasked.
*Arthur Schopenhauer*

Large offers and sturdy rejections are among the most common topics of falsehood.
*Samuel Johnson*

We pay a person the compliment of acknowledging his superiority whenever we lie to him.
*Samuel Butler*

The cruelest lies are often told in silence.
*Robert Louis Stevenson*

# M

MADNESS—MUSIC

## MADNESS

We are all born mad. Some remain so.
*Samuel Beckett*

The different sorts of madness are innumerable.
*Arabian proverb*

A man of gladness seldom falls into madness.

Every man is mad on some point.

Though this be madness, yet there is method in it.
*William Shakespeare*

Every madman thinks all other men mad.
*Latin proverb*

We must remember that every "mental" symptom is a veiled
cry of anguish. Against what? Against oppression, or what
the patient experiences as oppression. The oppressed speak
a million tongues.
*Thomas Szasz*

Schizophrenic behaviour is a special strategy that a person
invents in order to live in an unlivable situation.
*R. D. Laing*

## MAJORITY

One, on God's side, is a majority.
*Wendell Phillips*

The opinion of the majority is not the final proof of what is right.
*Schiller*

## MALICE

Malice hath a strong memory.

Malice must go under the disguise of plainness, or else it is
exposed.
*Marquess of Halifax*

## MAN

Show me a man with both feet on the ground and I'll show
you a man who can't put his pants on.
*Arthur K. Watson*

## MANAGEMENT

A good manager is a man who isn't worried about his own career but rather the careers of those who work for him.
*Henry S. M. Burns*

If you command wisely, you'll be obeyed cheerfully.
*Thomas Fuller*

The greatest administrators do not achieve production through constraints and limitations. They provide opportunities.
*Lao-tzu*

Never tell people how to do things. Tell them what to do, and they will surprise you with their ingenuity.
*George S. Patton*

Good management consists in showing average people how to do the work of superior people.
*John D. Rockefeller*

The ability to deal with people is as purchasable a commodity as sugar or coffee. And I pay more for that ability than for any other under the sun.
*John D. Rockefeller*

Lots of folks confuse bad management with destiny.
*Kin Hubbard*

## MANKIND

Man is equally incapable of seeing the nothingness from which he emerges and the infinity in which he is engulfed.
*Blaise Pascal*

It is easier to know man in general than to understand one man in particular.
*La Rochefoucauld*

Man's inhumanity to man makes countless thousands mourn!
*Robert Burns*

A man of words and not of deeds
Is like a garden full of weeds.

Man is the only animal that blushes. Or needs to.
*Mark Twain*

If man had created man he would be ashamed of his performance.
*Mark Twain*

Everyone has something in his nature which, if he were to express it openly, would of necessity give offence.
*Johann Goethe*

## MANNERS

Good manners are made up of petty sacrifices.

I don't recall your name, but your manners are familiar.
*Oliver Herford*

The test of good manners is to be patient with bad ones.
*Solomon Ibn Gabirol*

When a man is positively rude, it is as if he had cast off all his clothes and stood before us naked. Of course, like most people in this condition, he cuts a poor figure.
*Arthur Schopenhauer*

## MARKET

I dropped a lot of money in the market today. My shopping bag broke.

## MARRIAGE

All marriages are happy. It's the living together afterwards that causes all the trouble.

Marrying for money is the hardest way to earn it.

Marriage is a wonderful institution. If it weren't for marriage, husbands and wives would have to fight with perfect strangers.

To marry once is a duty, twice a folly, thrice is madness.
*Dutch proverb*

Husband and wife come to look alike at last.
*Oliver Wendell Holmes*

Only two things are necessary to keep one's wife happy. One is to let her think she is having her own way, and the other, to let her have it.
*Lyndon B. Johnson*

Married couples who love each other tell each other a thousand things without talking.
*Chinese proverb*

Seldom, or perhaps never, does a marriage develop into an individual relationship smoothly and without crises; there is no coming to consciousness without pain.
*Carl Jung*

What therefore God hath joined together, let not man put asunder.
*Matthew 19:6*

He that marries for wealth, sells his liberty.

Love is blind, but marriage restores its sight.
*G. C. Lichtenberg*

Very often the only thing that comes between a charming man and a charming woman is the fact that they are married to each other.
*Robert De Flers, Gaston Caillavet*

Keep thy eyes wide open before marriage, and half shut afterwards.
*Benjamin Franklin*

Marriage halves our griefs, doubles our joys, and quadruples our expenses.

Second marriage: Another instance of the triumph of hope over experience.
*Samuel Johnson*

A good marriage should be between a blind wife and a deaf husband.
*Michel de Montaigne*

When a man's friend marries, all is over between them.
*French proverb*

Marry in haste, and repent at leisure.
*Greek proverb*

Observe the mother and take the daughter.
*Turkish proverb*

For this cause shall a man leave his father and mother, and shall be joined unto his wife, and they two shall be one flesh.
*Ephesians 5:31*

I gravely doubt whether women ever were married by capture. I think they pretended to be; as they still do.
*G. K. Chesterton*

The most difficult year of marriage is the one you're in.
*Franklin P. Jones*

Marriage is our last, best chance to grow up.
*Joseph Barth*

A successful marriage is an edifice that must be rebuilt every day.
*André Maurois*

## MARTYR

There are as many martyrs for bad causes as for good ones.

The blood of the martyrs is the seed of the church.
*Tertullian*

## MASCARA

Laugh and the world laughs with you—cry and you streak your mascara.

## MASTER

He that is master must serve.

He that is master of himself will soon be master of others.

Masters should be sometimes blind and sometimes deaf.

One eye of the master sees more than ten of the servants'.

Masters' hints are commands.
*Italian proverb*

The master's face does more than the back of his head.
*Latin proverb*

Not everyone who sits in the seat of honor is master.
*Yiddish proverb*

## MATURITY

Maturity is the capacity to endure uncertainty.
*John Finley*

I believe that the sign of maturity is accepting deferred gratification.
*Peggy Cahn*

Grown up, and that is a terribly hard thing to do. It is much easier to skip it and go from one childhood to another.
*F. Scott Fitzgerald*

## MAXIM

A good maxim is never out of season.

Maxims are the condensed good sense of nations.

The maxims of men disclose their hearts.
*French proverb*

## MEANNESS

There are many things that we would throw away, if we were not afraid that others might pick them up.
*Oscar Wilde*

## MEANS

Use the means and God will give the blessing.

## MEASURE

Just scales and full measure injure no man.
*Chinese proverb*

Better twice measured than once wrong.
*Danish proverb*

You can't measure the whole world with your own yardstick.
*Yiddish proverb*

## MEDDLING

He who tastes every man's broth sometimes burns his mouth.
*Danish proverb*

## MEDICINE

Medicine has become so expensive that the only people who make house calls are burglars.

Most things get better by themselves. Most things, in fact, are better by morning.
*Lewis Thomas*

Wherever the art of medicine is loved, there also is love of humanity.
*Hippocrates*

An ounce of prevention is worth a pound of cure.

It is part of the cure to wish to be cured.
*Latin proverb*

## MEEK

They can be meek that have no other cause.
*William Shakespeare*

## MELANCHOLY

If there be a hell upon earth, it is to be found in the melancholy man's heart.
*Robert Burton*

## MEMORY

To improve your memory, lend people money.

Writing things down is the best secret of a good memory.

The Right Honorable gentleman is indebted to his memory for his jests and to his imagination for his facts.
*R. B. Sheridan*

It isn't so astonishing, the number of things that I can remember, as the number of things I can remember that aren't so.
*Mark Twain*

"The horror of that moment," the King went on, "I shall never, never forget!" "You will, though," the Queen said, "if you don't make a memorandum of it."
*Lewis Carroll*

Not the power to remember, but its very opposite, the power to forget, is a necessary condition for our existence.
*Sholem Asch*

What was hard to endure is sweet to recall. Good memories have ill judgments.

Memory of happiness makes misery woeful.

Sorrow remembered sweetens present joy.

That which is bitter to endure may be sweet to remember.

The true art of memory is the art of attention.

How sweet to remember the trouble that is past!
*Greek proverb*

In plucking the fruit of memory one runs the risk of spoiling its bloom.
*Joseph Conrad*

Memory is the cabinet of imagination, the treasury of reason, the registry of conscience, and the council chamber of thought.
*St. Basil*

## MERCY
Mercy to the criminal may be cruelty to the people.
*Arabian proverb*

Blessed are the merciful: for they shall obtain mercy.
*Matthew 5:7*

## MERRY
A merry companion on the road is as good as a nag.

Is any merry? Let him sing psalms.
*James 5:13*

It is good to be merry at dinner.

## MIDDLE AGE
A man has reached middle age when he is warned to slow down by his doctor, instead of the police.

Adolescence is when you think you'll live forever. Middle age is when you wonder how you've lasted so long.

You have reached middle age when all you exercise is caution.

Patience makes a woman beautiful in middle age.
*Elliot Paul*

The really frightening thing about middle age is the knowledge that you'll grow out of it.
*Doris Day*

## MIGHT

Where might is master, justice is servant.
*German proverb*

## MIND

Having a hole in the head doesn't always indicate an open mind.

Many people think they have an open mind when it is really their mouth.

Minds, like streams, may be so broad that they're shallow.

Strength is a matter of the made-up mind.
*John Beecher*

A vacant mind is open to all suggestions, as a hollow mountain returns all sounds.
*Chinese proverb*

A strong body makes a mind strong.

In the long run the sword is beaten by the mind.
*Napoleon Bonaparte*

It is good to rub and polish our minds against those of others.
*Michel de Montaigne*

A noble mind is free to all men.
*Latin proverb*

A sick mind cannot endure any harshness.
*Latin proverb*

Pain of mind is worse than pain of body.
*Latin proverb*

To relax the mind is to lose it.
*Latin proverb*

The mind is like the stomach. It is not how much you put into it that counts, but how much it digests.
*Albert Jay Nock*

## MINUTE
Take care of the minutes, and the hours will take care of themselves.

## MIRACLE
Miracles serve not to convert, but to condemn.
*Blaise Pascal*

I should not be a Christian but for the miracles.
*St. Augustine*

## MIRROR
The best mirror is an old friend.

## MIRTH
An ounce of mirth is worth a pound of sorrow.

Mirth makes the banquet sweet.

## MISCHIEF
He that mischief hatcheth, mischief catcheth.

He prepares evil for himself who plots mischief for others.
*Latin proverb*

## MISER
Nowadays a miser is one who lives within his income.

The miser and the pig are of no use to the family till dead.

To beg of the miser is to dig a trench in the sea.
*Turkish proverb*

## MISERY

He that is down need fear no fall.
*John Bunyan*

Fire tries gold, misery tries brave men.
*Seneca*

Misery loves company, but company does not reciprocate.
*Addison Mizner*

## MISFORTUNE

He took his misfortune like a man. He blamed it on his wife.

Fortune knocks once, but misfortune has more patience.

Misfortunes never come alone.

By speaking of our misfortunes we often relieve them.
*French proverb*

Misfortunes come on horseback and depart on foot.
*French proverb*

He who cannot bear misfortune is truly unfortunate.
*Greek proverb*

It is the nature of mortals to kick a man when he is down.
*Greek proverb*

Misfortune is friendless.
*Greek proverb*

Misfortune does not always come to injure.
*Italian proverb*

Another's misfortune does not cure my pain.
*Portuguese proverb*

When misfortune sleeps, let no one wake her.
*Spanish proverb*

## MISS

An inch in a miss is as good as a mile.

## MISTAKES

He who makes no mistakes makes nothing.

Mistakes are often the best teachers. The shortest mistakes are always the best.
*French proverb*

Any man may make a mistake; none but a fool will persist in it.
*Latin proverb*

To err is human, but when the eraser wears out ahead of the pencil, you're overdoing it.
*J. Jenkins*

Great services are not canceled by one act or by one single error.
*Benjamin Disraeli*

Men are men, they needs must err.
*Euripides*

Most men would rather be charged with malice than with making a blunder.
*Josh Billings*

It is very easy to forgive others their mistakes. It takes more gut and gumption to forgive them for having witnessed your own.
*Jessamyn West*

Things could be worse. Suppose your errors were counted and published every day, like those of a baseball player.
*Anonymous*

Even brute beasts and wandering birds do not fall into the same traps or net twice.
*St. Ambrose*

Don't ever promote a man who hasn't made some big mistakes—you'll be promoting a man who hasn't done much.
*Herbert H. Dow*

The greatest mistake you can make in life is to be continually fearing you will make one.
*Elbert Hubbard*

Great men have been characterized by the greatness of their mistakes as well as by the greatness of their achievements.
*Abraham Myerson*

## MOCKERY

Mocking is catching.

## MODERATION

Even moderation ought not to be practiced to excess.
*Anonymous*

Give me neither poverty nor riches.
*Proverbs 30:8*

He who wishes to travel far spares his steed.
*French proverb*

The golden rule in life is moderation in all things.
*Latin proverb*

## MODESTY

No one can boast of his modesty.

Though modesty be a virtue, bashfulness is a vice.

Rare is agreement between beauty and modesty.
*Latin proverb*

## MONEY

Money doesn't grow on trees; you've got to beat the bushes for it.

Money talks, but it doesn't always talk sense.

The buck stopped before it got here.

Money burns a hole in the pocket.

The love of someone else's money is the root of all evil.

Two can live as cheaply as one, but only half as long.

By the time a man has money to burn, the fire has gone out.

Money can't buy everything—poverty, for example.

For the first time in my life I've got money to burn and let's
face it—it's cheaper than fuel.

When money speaks, the truth is silent.
*Russian proverb*

The love of money is the root of all evil.
*1 Timothy 6:10*

Money is like a sixth sense, and you can't make use of the other five without it.
*W. Somerset Maugham*

The darkest hour of any man's life is when he sits down to plan how to get money without earning it.
*Horace Greeley*

I never been in no situation where havin' money made it any worse.
*Clinton Jones*

How do you make a million? You start with $900,000.
*Stephen Lewis*

When you have told anyone you have left him a legacy, the only decent thing to do is to die at once.
*Samuel Butler*

With money in your pocket, you are wise, and you are handsome, and you sing well too.
*Jewish proverb*

A good mind possesses a kingdom: a great fortune is a great slavery.
*Seneca*

Money talks. It says, good-bye.
*Anonymous*

Those who despise money will eventually sponge off their friends.
*Chinese proverb*

Money, if it does not bring you happiness, will at least help you to be miserable in comfort.
*Lord Mancroft*

A fool and his money are soon parted.

A fool may make money, but it needs a wise man to spend it.

Money is to be respected; one of the worst things you can do is handle another person's money without respect for how hard it was to earn.
*T. Boone Pickens Jr.*

God send you more wit and me more money.

If you want to know what God thinks of money, look at the people he gives it to.

Money is a good servant but a bad master.

The love of money and the love of learning seldom meet.

The price we pay for money is paid in liberty.

Would you know what money is? Go borrow some.

It is easier to make money than to keep it.
*Yiddish proverb*

There is one advantage of being poor—a doctor will cure you faster.
*Kin Hubbard*

Ready money is Aladdin's lamp.
*Lord Byron*

## MONEY-GRABBER
A money-grabber is anyone who grabs more money than you can.

## MONOPOLIES
Monopolies are like babies: nobody likes them until they have got one of their own.
*Lord Mancroft*

## MONUMENT
Those only deserve a monument who do not need one.

I would rather have men ask why I have no statue than why I have one.
*Greek proverb*

## MORALIST

Wink at small faults; for thou hast great ones.
*Thomas Fuller*

He who says there is no such thing as an honest man, you may be sure is himself a knave.
*Bishop Berkeley*

## MORALITY

To give a man full knowledge of true morality, I would send him to no other book than the New Testament.
*John Locke*

In any assembly the simplest way to stop transacting business and split the ranks is to appeal to a principle.
*Jacques Barzun*

## MORTICIAN

A mortician is a person who covers the doctor's mistakes.

## MOTHER

A mother is a person who, seeing there are only four pieces of pie for five people, promptly announces she never did care for pie.

One mother can take care of ten children, but ten children can't take care of one mother.

God could not be everywhere and therefore he made mothers.
*Hebrew proverb*

The mother-in-law remembers not that she was a daughter-in-law.
*Spanish proverb*

## MOTIVATION

Lord, grant that I may always desire more than I can accomplish.
*Michelangelo*

Men are not only bad from good motives, but also often good from bad motives.
*G. K. Chesterton*

## MOUNTAIN

If you don't scale the mountain, you can't view the plain.
*Chinese proverb*

## MOUTH

Some people think they have an open mind when it is really their mouth.

Mouth shut and eyes open.
*Italian proverb*

## MUD

He who is in the mud likes to pull another into it.
*Spanish proverb*

## MUSIC

One cannot judge "Lohengrin" from a first hearing, and I certainly do not intend to hear it a second time.
*Gioacchino A. Rossini*

Opera is when a guy gets stabbed in the back and instead of bleeding he sings.
*Ed Gardner*

Music hath charms to soothe the savage beast.
*William Congreve*

# N

NAME—NOSEBLEED

## NAME

A good name is rather to be chosen than great riches.
*Proverbs 22:1*

A good name keeps its luster in the dark.

Who has a bad name is half hanged.
*Italian proverb*

The beginning of wisdom is to call things by their right names.
*Chinese proverb*

Nicknames stick to people, and the most ridiculous are the most adhesive.
*Thomas Haliburton*

## NATURE

When elephants fight it is the grass that suffers.
*African saying*

Man is a complex being: he makes deserts bloom and lakes die.
*Gil Stern*

For the earth is the Lord's, and the fulness thereof.
*1 Corinthians 10:26*

The heavens declare the glory of God; and the firmament sheweth his handiwork.
*Psalm 19:1*

Bees are not as busy as we think they are. They just can't buzz any slower.
*Kin Hubbard*

Nature, to be commanded, must be obeyed.
*Francis Bacon*

## NECESSITY

Necessity makes even the timid brave.
*Sallust*

## NEGOTIATION

Don't ever slam the door; you might want to go back.
*Don Herold*

Enter into negotiations with the intention of creating an agreement that will allow both parties to achieve their essential goals.
*Tom Hopkins*

When I'm getting ready to reason with a man, I spend one-third of my time thinking about myself and what I am going to say—and two-thirds thinking about him and what he is going to say.
*Abraham Lincoln*

## NEIGHBORS

My neighbors are keeping me broke. They are always buying things I can't afford.

Summer must be over. My neighbor just returned my lawn furniture.

We make our friends; we make our enemies, but God makes our next-door neighbour.
*G. K. Chesterton*

## NEUROSIS

The psychotic person knows that two and two makes five and is perfectly happy about it; the neurotic person knows that two and two make four, but is terribly worried about it.
*Radio doctor*

Neurosis is always a substitute for legitimate suffering.
*Carl Jung*

## NEWS

As cold waters to a thirsty soul, so is good news from a far country.
*Proverbs 25:25*

Literature is news that stays news.
*Ezra Pound*

No news is good news.
*Italian proverb*

## NEWSPAPER

Remember, son, many a good story has been ruined by over-verification.
*James Gordon Bennett*

Don't be afraid to make a mistake, your readers might like it.
*William Randolph Hearst*

He had been kicked in the head by a mule when young, and believed everything he read in the Sunday papers.
*George Ade*

## NOBILITY

Send your noble blood to market and see what it will bring.
*Thomas Fuller*

## NONVIOLENCE

Passive resistance is an all-sided sword; it can be used anyhow; it blesses him who uses it and him against whom it is used without drawing a drop of blood; it produces far-reaching results. It never rusts and cannot be stolen. Competition between passive resisters does not exhaust them. The sword of passive resistance does not require a scabbard and one cannot be forcibly dispossessed of it.
*Mahatma Gandhi*

## NOSE

Keep your nose out of another's mess.
*Danish proverb*

## NOSEBLEED

The best way to avoid a nosebleed is to keep out of other people's business.

# O

OATH—ORIGINALITY

## OATH

A true word needs no oath.
*Turkish proverb*

## OBEDIENCE

Obedience alone gives the right to command.
*Ralph Waldo Emerson*

Learn to obey before you command.
*Greek proverb*

When a gentleman hath learned to obey he will grow very much fitter to command; his own memory will advise him not to command too rigorous punishments.
*George Savile, Lord Halifax*

It is much safer to obey than to rule.
*Thomas à Kempis*

## OBSCENITY

If it's illegal to send obscene material through the mail—how come my electric bill gets through?

## OBSERVATION

Every man is a volume if you know how to read him.
*William Channing*

The eyes believe themselves; the ears believe other people.
*German proverb*

You can observe a lot just by watching.
*Yogi Berra*

The ear tends to be lazy, craves the familiar and is shocked by the unexpected; the eye, on the other hand, tends to be impatient, craves the novel and is bored by repetition.
*W. H. Auden*

To him that watches, everything is revealed.
*Italian proverb*

Each one sees what he carries in his heart.
*Johann Goethe*

He alone is an acute observer, who can observe minutely
without being observed.
*Johann Kaspar Lavater*

When you have a taste for exceptional people you always end
up meeting them everywhere.
*Pierre Mac Orlan*

Every man is bound to leave a story better than he found it.
*Mrs. Humphry Ward*

## OBSTACLES

If you want a place in the sun, you've got to expect a few
blisters.
*Anonymous*

## OBSTINACY

The difference between perseverance and obstinacy is that
perseverance means a strong will and obstinacy means a
strong won't.
*Lord Dundee*

## OCCUPATION

Jack of all trades is master of none.

## OLD AGE

I find it hard to make ends meet—ends like my fingers and
toes.

You know you're getting old when all the names in your little
black book are doctors.

Old age is when you know all the answers but nobody asks
you the questions.

First you are young; then you are middle-aged; then you are
old; then you are wonderful.
*Lady Diana Cooper*

I want to die young at a ripe old age.
*Ashley Montagu*

An old man in a house is a good sign.

You know you're getting old when you've got money to burn, but the fire's gone out.
*Hy Gardner*

## OLD-TIMER

You're an old-timer if you can remember when the most popular family on the block was the one with the TV set.

You're an old-timer if you remember when a baby-sitter was called a mother.

An old-timer is one who remembers when we counted our blessings instead of our calories.

## OPERATION

A minor operation is one performed on someone else.

## OPINIONS

Some people fall for everything and stand for nothing.

Its name is Public Opinion. It is held in reverence. It settles everything. Some think it is the voice of God.
*Mark Twain*

Birds are taken with pipes that imitate their own voices, and men with those sayings that are most agreeable to their own opinions.
*Samuel Butler*

The right to be heard does not automatically include the right to be taken seriously.
*Hubert Humphrey*

It is difference of opinion that makes horse-races.
*Mark Twain*

Opinion is determined by feeling, not by intellect.

The man who never alters his opinion is like standing water, and breeds reptiles of the mind.
*William Blake*

He thinks by infection, catching an opinion like a cold.
*John Ruskin*

If you must tell me your opinions, tell me what you believe in.
I have plenty of doubts of my own.
*Johann Goethe*

He that never changes his opinions, never corrects his mistakes,
and will never be wiser on the morrow than he is today.
*Tryon Edwards*

The rule is perfect: In all matters of opinion our adversaries
are insane.
*Mark Twain*

If you laid all of man's opinions end to end, there would be
no end.

## OPPORTUNITY

An opportunist can hand out baloney disguised as food for
thought.

Even when opportunity knocks, a man must get off his seat to
open the door.

Opportunity knocks only once, but temptation bangs on the
door for years.

When opportunity knocks at the door, most people are out in
the backyard looking for four-leaf clovers.

Why are opportunities always bigger going than coming?

The sign on the door of opportunity reads "Push."

Golden opportunities are not found in the realm of slumber.

Plough deep while sluggards sleep.
*Benjamin Franklin*

If you're looking for a big opportunity, seek out a big problem.

A wise man will make more opportunities than he finds.
*Francis Bacon*

In the middle of difficulty lies opportunity.
*Albert Einstein*

God gives the nuts, but he does not crack them.
*German proverb*

Opportunities are seldom labeled.

I despise making the most of one's time. Half of the pleasures of life consist of the opportunities one has neglected.
*Oliver Wendell Holmes*

No great man ever complains of want of opportunity.
*Ralph Waldo Emerson*

## OPPOSITION

Don't be afraid of opposition. Remember, a kite rises against, not with, the wind.
*Hamilton Mabie*

Men are not against you; they are merely for themselves.
*Jan Christian Smuts*

No Government can long be secure without a formidable Opposition.
*Benjamin Disraeli*

## OPTIMIST

An optimist is a man who, instead of feeling sorry he cannot pay his bills, is glad he is not one of his creditors.

Optimism: A cheerful frame of mind that enables a tea kettle to sing though in hot water up to its nose.

Since the house is on fire, let us warm ourselves.
*Italian saying*

If you count the sunny and the cloudy days of the whole year, you will find that the sunshine predominates.

A cheerful resignation is always heroic, but no phase of life is so pathetic as a forced optimism.
*Elbert Hubbard*

An optimist is one who believes that a fly is looking for a way to get out.

An optimist is one who sends a package by parcel post and marks it "rush."

## ORATORY

He is a good orator who convinces himself.

## ORIGINALITY

There is nothing new under the sun.
*Ecclesiastes 1:9 (NKJV)*

Originality is simply a pair of fresh eyes.
*Thomas W. Higginson*

I invent nothing. I rediscover.
*Auguste Rodin*

The more intelligent a man is, the more originality he discovers
in men. Ordinary people see no difference between men.
*Blaise Pascal*

Why can't somebody give us a list of things that everybody
thinks and nobody says, and another list of things that everybody says and nobody thinks?
*Oliver Wendell Holmes*

# P

PAIN—PUNISHMENT

## PAIN

Those who do not feel pain seldom think that it is felt.
*Samuel Johnson*

## PARANOIA

Even a paranoid can have enemies.
*Henry Kissinger*

## PARENTHOOD

Parents can give everything but common sense.
*Yiddish proverb*

He who takes the child by the hand takes the mother by the heart.
*German proverb*

To bring up a child in the way he should go, travel that way yourself once in a while.
*Josh Billings*

Train up a child in the way he should go, and when he is old he will not depart from it.
*Proverbs 22:6 (NKJV)*

## PARKING

I solved the parking problem; I bought a parked car.

## PARTING

Departure should be sudden.
*Benjamin Disraeli*

A man never knows how to say good-bye; a woman never knows when to say it.
*Helen Rowland*

To part is to die a little.
*French proverb*

## PARTNERSHIP

When two friends have a common purse, one sings and the other weeps.
*Anonymous*

A friendship founded on business is better than a business founded on friendship.
*John D. Rockefeller Jr.*

The man who goes alone can start today; but he who travels with another must wait till that other is ready.
*Henry David Thoreau*

Two captains sink the ship.
*Turkish proverb*

Every sin is the result of a collaboration.
*Stephen Crane*

## PASSION

The end of passion is the beginning of repentance.

All passions exaggerate: it is only because they exaggerate that they are passions.

In the human heart new passions are forever being born; the overthrow of one almost always means the rise of another.
*La Rochefoucauld*

It is difficult to overcome one's passions, and impossible to satisfy them.
*Marguerite de La Sabliere*

Govern your passions, or they will govern you.
*Latin proverb*

## PAST

Nothing is certain except the past.
*Latin proverb*

## PATH

Every path hath a puddle.

## PATIENCE

Never think that God's delays are God's denials. Hold on; hold fast; hold out. Patience is genius.
*Count de Buffon*

A handful of patience is worth more than a bushel of brains.
*Dutch proverb*

Patience is bitter but its fruit is sweet.
*French proverb*

Patience has its limits. Take it too far and it's cowardice.
*George Jackson*

Patience is the best medicine there is for a sick man.

Patience is a drink to kill the Giant Despair.

He that can have patience can have what he will.
*Benjamin Franklin*

Rome was not built in a day.
*Latin proverb*

A watched pot never boils.

## PATRIOTISM
A man who is good enough to shed his blood for his country is good enough to be given a square deal afterwards.
*Theodore Roosevelt*

## PEACE
Peace won by compromise is usually a short-lived achievement.
*Winfield Scott*

To be prepared for war is one of the most effectual means of preserving peace.
*George Washington*

One sword keeps another in the sheath.
*George Herbert*

Blessed are the peacemakers: for they shall be called the children of God.
*Matthew 5:9*

The peace of God, which passeth all understanding . . .
*Philippians 4:7*

## PEN

If you give me six lines written by the hand of the most honest of men, I will find something in them which will hang him.
*A. Richelieu*

A sword does less hurt than a pen.

The pen is mightier than the sword.

## PENNY

Penny wise and pound foolish.

## PEOPLE

The Lord prefers common-looking people. That is the reason he made so many of them.
*Abraham Lincoln*

When people don't want to come, nothing will stop them.
*Sol Hurok*

When people are free to do as they please, they usually imitate each other.
*Eric Hoffer*

It is easy to see through people who make spectacles of themselves.

There are now three classes of people: the haves, the have-nots, and the charge-its.

## PERSEVERANCE

The waters wear the stones.
*Job 14:19*

It is a long road from conception to completion.
*Moliere*

Victory belongs to the most persevering.
*Napoleon Bonaparte*

A man can stand almost anything except a succession of ordinary days.
*Johann Goethe*

Men fail much oftener from want of perseverance than from want of talent.
*William Cobbett*

Even the woodpecker owes his success to the fact that he uses his head and keeps pecking away until he finishes the job he starts.
*Coleman Cox*

Fall seven times, stand up eight.
*Japanese proverb*

We can do anything we want to do if we stick to it long enough.
*Helen Keller*

Persevere and never fear.

Slow and steady wins the race.

## PERSISTENCE

So long as there is breath in me, that long will I persist. For now I know one of the greatest principles of success; if I persist long enough I will win.
*Og Mandino*

Success seems to be largely a matter of hanging on after others have let go.
*William Feather*

Never, never, never, never give up.
*Winston Churchill*

If at first you don't succeed, try, try again.

## PERSUASION

Soft words are hard arguments.
*Thomas Fuller*

People are generally better persuaded by the reasons which they have themselves discovered than by those which have come into the mind of others.
*Blaise Pascal*

One of the best ways to persuade others is with your ears—
by listening to them.
*Dean Rusk*

By long forbearing is a prince persuaded.
*Proverbs 25:15*

There is a holy, mistaken zeal in politics, as well as religion.
By persuading others we convince ourselves.
*Junius*

## PESSIMISM

If it weren't for the optimist, the pessimist wouldn't know how
happy he isn't.

How happy are the pessimists! What joy is theirs when they
have proved there is no joy.
*Marie Eber-Eschenbach*

Pessimist—one who, when he has the choice of two evils,
chooses both.
*Oscar Wilde*

My pessimism goes to the point of suspecting the sincerity of
the pessimists.
*Jean Rostand*

A pessimist builds slums in the air.

A pessimist is a man with a difficulty for every solution.

A pessimist feels bad when he feels good for fear he'll feel
worse when he feels better.

A pessimist is a person to borrow money from—he never
expects to be repaid.

## PHILANTHROPY

Blessed is he that considereth the poor.
*Psalm 41:1*

## PHILOSOPHY

There was never yet philosopher that could endure the tooth-
ache patiently.
*William Shakespeare*

All philosophy lies in two words: sustain and abstain.
*Epictetus*

I've developed a new philosophy—I only dread one day at a time.
*Charles M. Schulz*

I have a simple philosophy. Fill what's empty. Empty what's full.
And scratch where it itches.
*Alice Roosevelt Longworth*

There is only one thing that a philosopher can be relied on to
do, and that is, to contradict other philosophers.
*William James*

A blind man in a dark room looking for a black hat which is
not there.
*Anonymous*

## PIPER
You will have to pay the piper.

## PLAGIARISM

Whatever is well said by another, is mine.
*Seneca*

Plagiarists have, at least, the merit of preservation.
*Benjamin Disraeli*

A certain awkwardness marks the use of borrowed thoughts;
but as soon as we have learned what to do with them, they
become our own.
*Ralph Waldo Emerson*

## PLANNING
Act quickly, think slowly.
*Greek proverb*

Dig a well before you are thirsty.
*Chinese proverb*

## PLAY
The play was so bad, even the ushers hissed.
*Burle Wilkinson*

## PLEASE
He that all men will please shall never find ease.

## PLEASURE
The great pleasure in life is doing what people say you cannot do.
*Walter Bagehot*

He that loveth pleasure shall be a poor man.
*Proverbs 21:17*

That man is richest whose pleasures are the cheapest.
*Henry David Thoreau*

After pleasant scratching comes painful smarting.
*Danish proverb*

Pleasure makes the hours seem short.

Pleasure is the greatest incentive to vice.
*Greek proverb*

## PLENTY
My cup runneth over.
*Psalm 23:5*

## PLUMBER
You think you have problems? We have a plumber who no longer makes house calls.

## POLITICS
The essential ingredient of politics is timing.
*Pierre Elliott Trudeau*

Practical politics consists in ignoring facts.
*Henry Adams*

Congress is so strange. A man gets up to speak and says nothing. Nobody listens, then everybody disagrees.
*Boris Marshalov*

What counts is not necessarily the size of the dog in the fight—it's the size of the fight in the dog.
*Dwight D. Eisenhower*

Someone asked me . . . how I felt and I was reminded of a story that a fellow townsman of ours used to tell—Abraham Lincoln. They asked him how he felt once after an unsuccessful election. He said he felt like a little boy who had stubbed his toe in the dark. He said that he was too old to cry, but it hurt too much to laugh.
*Adlai Stevenson*

Once upon a time my political opponents honored me as possessing the fabulous intellectual and economic power by which I created a worldwide depression all by myself.
*Herbert Hoover*

Dirksen's Three Laws of Politics:
1. Get elected.
2. Get re-elected.
3. Don't get mad, get even.

Deep down he is shallow.
*Political saying*

Politics is more dangerous than war, for in war you are only killed once.
*Winston Churchill*

One fifth of the people are against everything all the time.
*Robert F. Kennedy*

You can fool too many of the people too much of the time.
*James Thurber*

One of the surest ways of killing a tree is to lay bare its roots. It is the same with institutions. We must not be too ready to disinter the origins of those we wish to preserve. All beginnings are small.
*Joseph Joubert*

I claim not to have controlled events, but confess plainly that events have controlled me.
*Abraham Lincoln*

Greater love hath no man than this, that he lay down his friends for his political life.
*Jeremy Thorpe*

Few politicians die, and none resign.
*Thomas Jefferson*

I have been driven many times to my knees by the overwhelming conviction that I had nowhere else to go. My own wisdom, and that of all about me seemed insufficient for the day.
*Abraham Lincoln*

More men have been elected between Sundown and Sunup than ever were elected between Sunup and Sundown.
*Will Rogers*

Macdonald's Law: Never write a letter if you can help it, and never destroy one.
*John A. Macdonald*

I'm not an old, experienced hand at politics. But I am now seasoned enough to have learned that the hardest thing about any political campaign is how to win without proving that you are unworthy of winning.
*Adlai Stevenson*

Never retract, never explain, never apologize—get the thing done and let them howl.
*Nellie McClung*

## POLLUTION
Before pollution, people used to get airsick only on planes.

## POOR
The poor you will always have with you.
*Matthew 26:11 (NIV)*

The rich would have to eat money, but luckily the poor provide food.
*Russian proverb*

## POPULARITY
Avoid popularity if you would have peace.
*Abraham Lincoln*

## POSITION
He sits not sure that sits too high.

## POSITIVISM

A single sunbeam is enough to drive away many shadows.
*St. Francis of Assisi*

## POSSESSION

As having nothing, and yet possessing all things.
*2 Corinthians 6:10*

No man can swim ashore and carry his baggage with him.
*Latin proverb*

The least of things with a meaning is worth more in life than
the greatest of things without it.
*Carl Jung*

A man's life consisteth not in the abundance of the things
which he possesseth.
*Luke 12:15*

Inanimate objects are classified scientifically into three major
categories—those that don't work, those that break down, and
those that get lost.
*Russell Baker*

Every increased possession loads us with a new weariness.
*John Ruskin*

## POSSIBILITIES

Few men during their lifetime come anywhere near exhausting
the resources dwelling within them. There are deep wells of
strength that are never used.
*Richard E. Byrd*

## POTPOURRI

Some will always be above others. Destroy the inequality
today and it will appear again tomorrow.
*Ralph Waldo Emerson*

The turtle lays thousands of eggs without anyone knowing, but when the hen lays an egg, the whole country is
informed.
*Malaysian proverb*

## POWER

Lust of power is the strongest of all passions.
*Latin proverb*

## PRACTICE

Practice makes perfect.
*Latin proverb*

## PRAISE

The sweetest of all sounds is praise.
*Xenophon*

It is simpler and easier to flatter men than to praise them.
*Jean Paul Richter*

He who loves praise loves temptation.

He who praises everybody praises nobody.

Do you want to injure someone's reputation? Don't speak ill
of him, speak too well.
*Andre Siegfried*

None are more apt to praise others extravagantly than those
who desire to be praised themselves.
*Anonymous*

Among the smaller duties of life I hardly know any one more
important than that of not praising where praise is not due.
*Sydney Smith*

Get someone else to blow your horn and the sound will carry
twice as far.
*Will Rogers*

## PRAYER

The fewer the words, the better the prayer.
*Martin Luther*

I have lived to thank God that all my prayers have not been
answered.
*Jean Ingelow*

All things, whatsoever ye shall ask in prayer, believing, ye shall receive.
*Matthew 21:22*

And Satan trembles when he sees
The weakest saint upon his knees.
*William Cowper*

To pray well is the better half of study.
*Martin Luther*

Nothing costs so much as what is bought by prayers.
*Seneca*

Prayer does not change God, but it changes him who prays.
*S. A. Kierkegaard*

## PREACH

A good example is the best sermon.

An ounce of practice is worth a pound of preaching.

None preaches better than the ant, and she says nothing.

Practice yourself what you preach.
*Latin proverb*

He preaches well that lives well.
*Spanish proverb*

When I hear a man preach, I like to see him act as if he were fighting bees.
*Abraham Lincoln*

I preached as never sure to preach again,
And as a dying man to dying men.
*Richard Baxter*

Few sinners are saved after the first twenty minutes of a sermon.
*Mark Twain*

## PREJUDICE

He hears but half who hears one party only.
*Aeschylus*

Everyone is a prisoner of his own experiences. No one can eliminate prejudices—just recognize them.
*Edward R. Murrow*

## PREPAREDNESS
In fair weather prepare for foul.
*Thomas Fuller*

Forewarned, forearmed; to be prepared is half the victory.
*Spanish proverb*

## PRESIDENCY
No man will ever bring out of the Presidency the reputation which carries him into it.
*Thomas Jefferson*

My movements to the chair of government will be accompanied by feelings not unlike those of a culprit who is going to the place of his execution.
*George Washington*

Seriously, I do not think I am fit for the presidency.
*Abraham Lincoln*

Had I been chosen president again, I am certain I could not have lived another year.
*John Adams*

The four most miserable years of my life.
*John Adams*

Within the first few months I discovered that being a president is like riding a tiger. A man has to keep riding or be swallowed.
*Harry S. Truman*

I sit here all day trying to persuade people to do the things they ought to have sense enough to do without my persuading them . . . that's all the powers of the President amount to.
*Harry S. Truman*

The White House is the finest prison in the world.
*Harry S. Truman*

## PRESS

In old days men had the rack. Now they have the press.
*Oscar Wilde*

## PRETENSION

The only good in pretending is the fun we get out of fooling ourselves that we fool somebody.
*Booth Tarkington*

The hardest tumble a man can make is to fall over his own bluff.
*Ambrose Bierce*

## PREVENTION

An ounce of prevention is worth a pound of cure.

## PRICE

The highest price a man can pay for a thing is to ask for it.

## PRIDE

Pride goeth before destruction, and an haughty spirit before a fall.
*Proverbs 16:18*

Those who obstinately oppose the most widely-held opinions more often do so because of pride than lack of intelligence. They find the best places in the right seat already taken, and they do not want back seats.
*La Rochefoucauld*

When a proud man hears another praised, he feels himself injured.
*English proverb*

There is a paradox in pride: it makes some men ridiculous, but prevents others from becoming so.
*Charles Caleb Colton*

As proud as a pig with two tails.

There was one who thought himself above me, and he was above me until he had that thought.
*Elbert Hubbard*

## PRINCIPLES

The difficulty is to know conscience from self-interest.
*W. D. Howells*

## PRIVATE INTEREST

We must especially beware of that small group of selfish men who would clip the wings of the American Eagle in order to feather their own nests.
*Franklin D. Roosevelt*

## PROBLEMS

Think as you work, for in the final analysis your worth to your company comes not only in solving problems but in anticipating them.
*Herbert H. Ross*

Some people approach every problem with an open mouth.
*Adlai Stevenson*

I never take a problem to bed with me at night.
*Harry S. Truman*

## PROCRASTINATION

Often greater risk is involved in postponement than in making a wrong decision.
*Harry A. Hopf*

"One of these days" is none of these days.

Never put off till tomorrow what can be done today.

Procrastination is the thief of time.
*Edward Young*

Putting off an easy thing makes it hard, and putting off a hard one makes it impossible.
*George H. Lorimer*

## PRODIGY

An infant prodigy is a young child whose parents are highly imaginative.

## PROFANITY

Nothing is greater, or more fearful sacrilege than to prostitute
the great name of God to the petulancy of an idle tongue.
*Jeremy Taylor*

## PROFIT

It is a socialist idea that making profits is a vice; I consider
that the real vice is making losses.
*Winston Churchill*

When shallow critics denounce the profit motive inherent in
our system of private enterprise, they ignore the fact that it
is an economic support of every human right we possess and
without it, all rights would disappear.
*Dwight D. Eisenhower*

Profit is a must. There can be no security for any employee in any
business that doesn't make money. There can be no growth for
that business. There can be no opportunity for the individual to
achieve his personal ambitions unless his company makes money.
*Duncan C. Manzies*

## PROGRESS

After thousands of years, we have advanced to the point where
we bolt our doors and windows, turn on our burglar alarms—
while the jungle natives sleep in open-door huts.

I will go anywhere provided it is forward.
*David Livingstone*

Now here, you see, it takes all the running you can do to keep
in the same place. If you want to get somewhere else, you
must run at least twice as fast as that!
*Lewis Carroll*

Always remember that the soundest way to progress in any
organization is to help the man ahead of you to get promoted.
*L. S. Hamaker*

Every year it takes less time to fly across the Atlantic and more
time to drive to the office.
*Anonymous*

Once a man would spend a week patiently waiting if he missed a stage coach, but now he rages if he misses the first section of a revolving door.
*Simeon Strunsky*

Restlessness and discontent are the first necessities of progress.
*Thomas Edison*

The life and spirit of the American economy is progress and expansion.
*Harry S. Truman*

He who moves not forward goes backward.
*German proverb*

I have found some of the best reasons I ever had for remaining at the bottom simply by looking at the men at the top.
*Frank Moore Colby*

## PROHIBITION
Things forbidden have a secret charm.
*Greek proverb*

## PROMISCUITY
Like the bee its sting, the promiscuous leave behind them in each encounter something of themselves by which they are made to suffer.
*Cyril Connolly*

## PROMISE
A man apt to promise is apt to forget.

He loses his thanks who promises and delays.
*Latin proverb*

Many promises impair confidence.
*Latin proverb*

Don't put it in my ear, but in my hand.
*Russian proverb*

Promises may get friends, but it is performance that must nurse and keep them.
*Owen Feltham*

An acre of performance is worth the whole Land of Promise.
*James Howell*

Promises and pie-crust are made to be broken.
*Jonathan Swift*

## PROMOTION

Comrades, you have lost a good captain to make him an ill general.
*Michel de Montaigne*

## PROPAGANDA

The most dangerous of all falsehoods is a slightly distorted truth.
*G. C. Lichtenberg*

## PROPERTY

Property is the fruit of labor; property is desirable; it is a positive good in the world. That some should be rich shows that others may become rich and, hence, is just encouragement to industry and enterprise.
*Abraham Lincoln*

No man acquires property without acquiring with it a little arithmetic also.
*Ralph Waldo Emerson*

## PROPHET

A prophet is not without honour, save in his own country, and in his own house.
*Matthew 13:57*

## PROSPERITY

It requires a strong constitution to withstand repeated attacks of prosperity.
*J. L. Basford*

In the day of prosperity be joyful, but in the day of adversity consider.
*Ecclesiastes 7:14*

Prosperity is the surest breeder of insolence I know.
*Mark Twain*

## PROVERBS
A proverb is the wit of one and the wisdom of many.

Proverbs are the wisdom of the streets.

A proverb is a short sentence based on long experience.
*Spanish proverb*

## PROVIDENCE
The longer I live, the more convincing proofs I see of this truth, that God governs in the affairs of man; and if a sparrow cannot fall to the ground without his notice, is it probable that an empire can rise without his aid?
*Benjamin Franklin*

## PROVISION
Lay up for a rainy day.

## PRUDENCE
Don't count your chickens before they are hatched.
*Aesop*

A stitch in time saves nine.

He that goes barefoot must not plant thorns.

A prudent man does not make the goat his gardener.
*Hungarian proverb*

Don't call the bear "Uncle" till you are safe across the bridge.
*Turkish proverb*

It is by the goodness of God that in our country we have those three unspeakably precious things: freedom of speech, freedom of conscience, and the prudence never to practice either.
*Mark Twain*

## PRYING
He who is always prying has a dangerous life.
*Spanish proverb*

## PSYCHIATRY

A psychiatrist's couch is where you land when you go off your rocker.

A psychiatrist is the next man you start talking to after you start talking to yourself.

Psychiatry enables us to correct our faults by confessing our parents' shortcomings.
*Laurence J. Peter*

Psychoanalysis is confession without absolution.
*G. K. Chesterton*

The four-letter word for psychotherapy is *talk*.
*Anonymous*

When a billing clerk goes psycho, he hears strange invoices.

A psychopath is a path where a psycho walks up and down.

## PUBLIC

He who serves the public hath but a scurvy master.

If it has to choose who is to be crucified, the crowd will always save Barabbas.
*Jean Cocteau*

## PUNCTUALITY

Unfaithfulness in the keeping of an appointment is an act of clear dishonesty. You may as well borrow a person's money as his time.
*Horace Mann*

## PUNISHMENT

We are not punished for our sins, but by them.
*Elbert Hubbard*

QUALITY—QUOTATION

## QUALITY

Conceal a flaw, and the world will imagine the worst.
*Martial*

I think there is only one quality worse than hardness of heart, and that is softness of head.
*Theodore Roosevelt*

## QUESTION

A fool may ask more questions in an hour than a wise man can answer in seven years.
*English proverb*

It is not every question that deserves an answer.
*Publilius Syrus*

Never answer a question until it is asked.

The uncreative mind can spot wrong answers, but it takes a creative mind to spot wrong questions.
*A. Jay*

## QUIET

Better is a dry morsel, and quietness therewith, than an house full of sacrifices with strife.
*Proverbs 17:1*

## QUOTATION

I quote others only the better to express myself.
*Michel de Montaigne*

It is a good thing for an uneducated man to read books of quotations.
*Winston Churchill*

Quotations when engraved upon the memory give you good thoughts.
*Winston Churchill*

I often quote myself. It adds spice to my conversation.
*George Bernard Shaw*

R

RADICAL—RUST

## RADICAL

A radical is anyone whose opinions differ radically from mine.

## RADIO

A radio announcer is a person who works for the love of mike.

## RAIN

Rain is something that makes flowers grow and taxicabs disappear.

After the rain cometh the fair weather.
*Aesop*

It never rains but it pours.
*English proverb*

## RAINBOW

The way I see it, if you want the rainbow, you gotta put up with the rain.
*Dolly Parton*

## RAISE

Nowadays a raise enables a man to live the way he is already living.

## READING

If we encountered a man of rare intellect, we should ask him what books he read.
*Ralph Waldo Emerson*

There is hardly any grief that an hour's reading will not dissipate.
*L. de Montesquieu*

Where do I find all the time for not reading so many books?
*Karl Kraus*

A reader cannot be more rationally entertained than by comparing and drawing a parallel between his own private character and that of other persons.
*Joseph Addison*

Reading is to the mind what exercise is to the body.
*Richard Steele*

You may have tangible wealth untold;
Caskets of jewels and coffers of gold.
Richer than I you can never be—
I had a mother who read to me.
*Strickland Gillilan*

When we read we may not only be kings and live in palaces,
but, what is far better, we may transport ourselves to the
mountains or the seashore, and visit the most beautiful parts
of the earth, without fatigue, inconvenience, or expense.
*John Lubbock*

To read without reflecting is like eating without digesting.
*Edmund Burke*

He that loves reading has everything within his reach.
*William Godwin*

Through the years, I have often been asked, at conferences
and at together gatherings, "How do you get so much reading
done?" May I say here, again, that there is only one way to get
any reading done, and that is to read. Whatever reading I may
do, I do not deprive myself of needed sleep, and am always
in bed for at least eight hours every night; I do not withdraw
myself from society; and I am not a man free from obligations,
that is, I have been a minister or professor all my adult life,
and thus many hours of the day are not my own. There is only
one way to get any reading done, and that is to read. If one
does not wish to read, he will not read—but if he does not,
his ministry will be impoverished indeed.
*Wilbur Smith*

Many times the reading of a book has made the future of
a man.
*Ralph Waldo Emerson*

Employ your time in improving yourself by other men's
writings so that you shall come easily by what others have
labored hard for.
*Socrates*

In a very real sense, people who have read good literature have lived more than people who cannot or will not read. . . . It is not true that we have only one life to live; if we can read, we can live as many more lives and as many kinds of lives as we wish.
*S. I. Hayakawa*

The more we read the more we believe,
The more we believe the more we hope,
The more we hope the more we pray,
The more we pray the more we love,
The more we love the more we labor.
*Mrs. Charles E. Cowman*

Read the best books first, or you may not have a chance to read them at all.
*Henry David Thoreau*

There is a great deal of difference between the eager man who wants to read a book and the tired man who wants a book to read.
*G. K. Chesterton*

A man ought to read just as his inclination leads him; for what he reads as a task will do him little good.
*Samuel Johnson*

Education . . . has produced a vast population able to read but unable to distinguish what is worth reading.
*G. M. Trevelyan*

To read between the lines was easier than to follow the text.
*Henry James*

## REASON

When a man has not a good reason for doing a thing, he has one good reason for letting it alone.
*Sir Walter Scott*

We are usually convinced more easily by reasons we have found ourselves than by those which have occurred to others.
*Blaise Pascal*

He who will not reason, is a bigot; he who cannot is a fool;
and he who dares not, is a slave.
*William Drummond*

Come now, and let us reason together.
*Isaiah 1:18*

Never try to reason the prejudice out of a man. It was not
reasoned into him, and cannot be reasoned out.
*Sydney Smith*

The heart has its reasons which reason does not know.
*Blaise Pascal*

## REBELLION

Inferiors revolt in order that they may be equal, and equals
that they may be superior.
*Aristotle*

By gnawing through a dyke, even a rat may drown a nation.
*Edmund Burke*

## RECESSION

The recession hasn't hurt my family yet—we can still live
beyond our means.

## RECRUITMENT

When you hire people who are smarter than you are,
you prove you are smarter than they are.
*Robert H. Grant*

The first requisite in running a major corporation is the
ability to pick good people.
*Lee Iacocca*

## REFORM

It is never too late to mend.

Reform must come from within, not from without.
*James Gibbons*

Every reform was once a private opinion.
*Ralph Waldo Emerson*

To reform a man, you must begin with his grandmother.
*Victor Hugo*

## REGRET

If you board the wrong train, it is no use running along the
corridor in the other direction.
*Dietrich Bonhoeffer*

Of all the horrid, hideous notes of woe, sadder than owl songs
or the midnight blast, is that portentous phrase, "I told you so."
*Lord Byron*

Footfalls echo in the memory down the passage which we
did not take towards the door we never opened into the rose
garden.
*T. S. Eliot*

For all sad words of tongue or pen,
The saddest are these: "It might have been!"
*John Greenleaf Whittier*

Regret is an appalling waste of energy; you can't build on it;
it's only good for wallowing in.
*Katherine Mansfield*

## RELATIVE

The worst hatred is that of relatives.
*Tacitus*

## RELIGION

The worst moment for the atheist is when he is really thankful,
and has nobody to thank.
*Dante Gabriel Rossetti*

Man doth not live by bread only, but by every word that
proceedeth out of the mouth of the Lord doth man live.
*Deuteronomy 8:3*

If I was a nightingale I would sing like a nightingale; if a swan,
like a swan. But since I am a rational creature my role is to
praise God.
*Epictetus*

To lift up the hands in prayer gives God glory, but a man with a dungfork in his hand, a woman with a sloppail, gives him glory too. He is so great that all things give him glory if you mean they should.
*Gerard Manley Hopkins*

Live among men as if God beheld you; speak to God as if men were listening.
*Seneca*

Every miracle can be explained—after the event. Not because the miracle is no miracle, but because explanation is explanation.
*Franz Rosenzweig*

No kingdom has ever had as many civil wars as the kingdom of Christ.
*L. de Montesquieu*

To the frivolous Christianity is certainly not glad tidings, for it wishes first of all to make them serious.
*S. A. Kierkegaard*

Men never do evil so completely and cheerfully as when they do it from religious conviction.
*Blaise Pascal*

Men will wrangle for religion; write for it; fight for it; die for it; anything but live for it.
*C. C. Colton*

## REMEDY

If there be no remedy, why worry?
*Spanish proverb*

## REMORSE

Remorse is the pain of sin.
*Theodore Parker*

Repentance costs dear.
*French proverb*

## REPROACH

The sting of a reproach is the truth of it.

## REPROOF

Reprove not a scorner, lest he hate thee: rebuke a wise man, and he will love thee.
*Proverbs 9:8*

## REPUTATION

A good name is better than precious ointment.
*Ecclesiastes 7:1*

A good name is rather to be chosen than great riches.
*Proverbs 22:1*

## RESIGNATION

Naked came I out of my mother's womb, and naked shall I return thither: the LORD gave, and the LORD hath taken away; blessed be the name of the LORD.
*Job 1:21*

It seems that nothing ever gets to going good till there's a few resignations.
*Kin Hubbard*

## RESOLUTION

Never tell your resolution beforehand.

## RESPECT

There was no respect for youth when I was young, and now that I am old, there is no respect for age—I missed it coming and going.
*J. B. Priestly*

I don't know what a scoundrel is like, but I know what a respectable man is like, and it's enough to make one's flesh creep.
*J. M. de Maistre*

## RESPONSIBILITY

Everybody's business is nobody's business.
*Anonymous*

Am I my brother's keeper?
*Genesis 4:9*

I believe that every right implies a responsibility; every opportunity, an obligation; every possession, a duty.
*John D. Rockefeller*

To be a man is, precisely, to be responsible.
*Antoine de Saint-Exupéry*

The fault, dear Brutus, is not in our start, but in ourselves, that we are underlings.
*William Shakespeare*

The great developer is responsibility.
*Louis D. Brandeis*

Responsibility is the price of greatness.
*Winston Churchill*

Responsibilities gravitate to the person who can shoulder them.
*Elbert Hubbard*

You can't escape the responsibility of tomorrow by evading it today.
*Abraham Lincoln*

Responsibility is the thing people dread most of all. Yet it is the only thing in the world that develops us, gives us manhood or womanhood fibre.
*Frank Crane*

Every man must carry his own sack to the mill.
*Italian proverb*

If each one sweeps before his own door, the whole street is clean.
*Yiddish proverb*

## REST

Too much rest itself becomes a pain.
*Greek proverb*

Come unto me, all ye that labour and are heavy laden, and I will give you rest.
*Matthew 11:28*

## RESTAURANT

When you go in a restaurant, always ask for a table near a waiter.

## RESULTS

By their fruits ye shall know them.
*Matthew 7:20*

Well done is better than well said.
*Benjamin Franklin*

## RESURRECTION

For as in Adam all die, even so in Christ shall all be made alive.
*1 Corinthians 15:22*

## RETIREMENT

Two weeks is about the ideal length of time to retire.
*Alex Comfort*

Few men of action have been able to make a graceful exit at the appropriate time.
*Malcolm Muggeridge*

The best time to start thinking about your retirement is before the boss does.
*Anonymous*

## RETRIBUTION

Whatsoever a man soweth, that shall he also reap.
*Galatians 6:7*

Men must reap the things they sow.
*Percy B. Shelley*

## REVENGE

A man that studieth revenge keeps his own wounds green, which otherwise would heal and do well.
*Francis Bacon*

Thou shalt not avenge.
*Leviticus 19:18*

Vengeance is mine; I will repay, saith the Lord.
*Romans 12:19*

Living well is the best revenge.
*George Herbert*

Revenge proves its own executioner.

There's small revenge in words, but words may be greatly revenged.

To forget a wrong is the best revenge.

Revenge is a confession of pain.
*Latin proverb*

If you want to be revenged, hold your tongue.
*Spanish proverb*

## REVOLUTION
Every revolution was first a thought in one man's mind.
*Ralph Waldo Emerson*

## REWARD
No man, who continues to add something to the material, intellectual and moral well-being of the place in which he lives, is left long without proper reward.
*Booker T. Washington*

No person was ever honored for what he received. Honor has been the reward for what he gave.
*Calvin Coolidge*

## RICHES
A man is rich in proportion to the number of things he can afford to let alone.
*Henry David Thoreau*

Riches are gotten with pain, kept with care, and lost with grief.

A great fortune is a great slavery.
*Latin proverb*

Wealth lightens not the heart and care of man.
*Latin proverb*

Lay not up for yourselves treasures upon earth, where moth and rust doth corrupt, and where thieves break through and steal.
*Matthew 6:19*

It is the wretchedness of being rich that you have to live with rich people.
*Logan Pearsall Smith*

## RIDICULOUS
There is only one step from the sublime to the ridiculous.
*Napoleon Bonaparte*

## RIDING
He who knows the road can ride at full trot.
*Italian proverb*

## RIGHT
Two wrongs do not make a right.

There never was a cause yet, right or wrong, that ever wanted an advocate to defend it.
*Anonymous*

## RIGHTEOUSNESS
If there is righteousness in the heart, there will be beauty in character. If there is beauty in character, there will be harmony in the home. If there is harmony in the home, there will be order in the nation. If there is order in the nation, there will be peace in the world.
*Chinese proverb*

## RISK
Take calculated risks. That is quite different from being rash.
*George S. Patton*

Great successes never come without risks.
*Flavius Josephus*

Everything is sweetened by risk.

## RIVER

Where the river is deepest it makes least noise.
*Italian proverb*

## ROAD

It is a long road that has no turning.

What is the use of running, when you're on the wrong road?

## ROLLING

A rolling stone gathers no moss.

## ROSE

He who plants thorns must never expect to gather roses.
*Arabian proverb*

## RUIN

The road to ruin is always kept in good repair.
*Anonymous*

## RULERS

He was a wise fellow that, being bid to ask what he would of the king, desired he might know none of his secrets.
*William Shakespeare*

Though men in great positions are easily flattered, we are still more easily flattered when in their company.
*Marquis de Vauvenargues*

## RUMOR

"They say so" is half a lie.
*Thomas Fuller*

. . . tattlers also and busybodies, speaking things which they ought not.
*1 Timothy 5:13*

What some invent the rest enlarge.
*Jonathan Swift*

I know nothing swifter in life than the voice of rumor.
*Plautus*

Rumor is a great traveler.

## RUST
The tanned appearance of many Londoners is not sunburn—
it is rust.
*London Evening Standard*

**S**

SAFETY—SYSTEM

## SAFETY

It is better to be safe than sorry.
*American proverb*

He is safe from danger who is on guard even when safe.
*Latin proverb*

A ship in harbor is safe, but that is not what ships are built for.
*John A. Shedd*

Let the people know the truth and the country is safe.
*Abraham Lincoln*

## SALES

A man without a smiling face must not open a shop.
*Chinese proverb*

Every seller praises his wares.
*Yiddish proverb*

Good wares make a quick market.

Pleasing ware is half sold.

## SALES RESISTANCE

Sales resistance is the triumph of mind over patter.

## SALT

If the salt have lost his saltness, wherewith will ye season it?
*Mark 9:50*

## SATISFACTION

There's more credit and satisfaction in being a first-rate truck driver than a tenth-rate executive.
*B. C. Forbes*

## SCALD

Scald not your lips on another man's porridge.

## SCANDAL

It is at home, not in public, one washes his dirty linen.
*French proverb*

Scandal dies sooner of itself than we could kill it.
*Benjamin Rush*

## SCHOLARS
He not only overflowed with learning, but stood in the slop.
*Sydney Smith*

## SCIENCE
Enough research will tend to support your theory.
*Anonymous*

## SCRATCH
I scratch where it itches.

## SECRETS
There are two kinds of secrets: one is not worth keeping, and the other is too good to keep.

Most people can keep a secret. It's the ones they tell it to that can't.

There is a skeleton in every house.
*Anonymous*

To keep your secret is wisdom; but to expect others to keep it is folly.
*Samuel Johnson*

I usually get my stuff from people who promised somebody else that they would keep it a secret.
*Walter Winchell*

Secrets are things we give to others to keep for us.
*Elbert Hubbard*

A secret is a weapon and a friend.

He who tells a secret is another's servant.

When a secret is revealed, it is the fault of the man who confided it.
*French proverb*

Three may keep a secret if two of them are dead.

If you would keep your secret from an enemy, tell it not to a friend.

Sooner will men hold fire in their mouths than keep a secret.
*Latin proverb*

Confide a secret to a dumb man, and he will speak.
*Russian proverb*

He who keeps his own secret avoids much mischief.
*Spanish proverb*

After nine months the secret comes out.
*Yiddish proverb*

Nothing is so burdensome as a secret.
*French proverb*

Even in your thought, do not curse the king, nor in your bedchamber curse the rich; for a bird of the air will carry your voice, or some winged creature tell the matter.
*Ecclesiastes 10:20 (RSV)*

All charming people have something to conceal, usually their total dependence on the appreciation of others.
*Cyril Connolly*

That I, or any man, should tell everything of himself, I hold to be impossible. Who could endure to own the doing of a mean thing? Who is there that has done none?
*Anthony Trollope*

You can take better care of your secret than another can.
*Ralph Waldo Emerson*

Nobody will keep the thing he hears to himself, and nobody will repeat just what he hears and no more.
*Seneca*

## SECURITY

Security is mostly a superstition. It does not exist in nature, nor do the children of men as a whole experience it. Avoiding danger is no safer in the long run than outright exposure. Life is either a daring adventure, or nothing.
*Helen Keller*

In no direction that we turn do we find ease or comfort. If we are honest and if we have the will to win we find only danger, hard work and iron resolution.
*Wendell K. Willkie*

## SEEM
Things are seldom what they seem.

## SELF
We judge ourselves by our motives and others by their actions.
*Dwight Morrow*

Blessed are they who heal us of self-despisings. Of all services which can be done to man, I know of none more precious.
*William Hale White*

## SELF-CONFIDENCE
Be always sure you're right, then go ahead.
*Davy Crockett*

The history of the world is full of men who rose to leadership, by sheer force of self-confidence, bravery, and tenacity.
*Mahatma Gandhi*

## SELF-CONTROL
He is strong who conquers others; he who conquers himself is mighty.
*Lao-Tzu*

## SELF-DEPENDENCE
Every tub must stand on its own bottom.

## SELF-DEPRECATION
He that makes himself dirt is trod on by the swine.

## SELF-DESTRUCTION
But I do nothing upon myself, and yet I am mine own Executioner.
*John Donne*

## SELF-DOUBT

Wrongs are often forgiven, but contempt never is. Our pride remembers it forever.
*Lord Chesterfield*

Many would be cowards if they had courage enough.
*Thomas Fuller*

It is easy—terribly easy—to shake a man's faith in himself. To take advantage of that to break a man's spirit is devil's work.
*Thomas Morell*

No man can make you feel inferior without your consent.

## SELF-ESTEEM

Every new adjustment is a crisis in self-esteem.
*Eric Hoffer*

## SELF-HELP

He that performs his own errand, saves his messenger's hire.
*Danish proverb*

Paddle your own canoe.

## SELF-IMAGE

Nothing is more depressing than the conviction that one is not a hero.
*George Moore*

## SELF-IMPROVEMENT

There is no use whatever trying to help people who do not help themselves. You cannot push anyone up a ladder unless he be willing to climb himself.
*Andrew Carnegie*

## SELF-KNOWLEDGE

Lord, deliver me from myself.

Almost every man wastes part of his life in attempts to display qualities which he does not possess, and to gain applause which he cannot keep.
*Samuel Johnson*

Up to a certain point every man is what he thinks he is.
*F. H. Bradley*

## SELF-LOVE

Self-love is the greatest of all flatterers.
*La Rochefoucauld*

He that considers how little he dwells upon the condition of others will learn how little the attention of others is attracted by himself.
*Samuel Johnson*

Everybody has his own theatre, in which he is manager, actor, prompter, playwright, scene-shifter, boxkeeper, doorkeeper, all in one, and audience into the bargain.
*Julius Hare*

We are so vain that we even care for the opinion of those we don't care for.
*Maria Ebner-Eschenbach*

We all think we are exceptional, and are surprised to find ourselves criticized just like anyone else.
*Comtesse Diane*

None so empty, as those who are full of themselves.
*Benjamin Whichcote*

The book written against fame and learning has the author's name on the title-page.
*Ralph Waldo Emerson*

## SELF-PRAISE

Let another man praise thee, and not thine own mouth.
*Proverbs 27:2*

Self-praise stinks in the nostrils.

## SELF-RELIANCE

Chop your own wood, and it will warm you twice.
*Henry Ford Sr.*

## SELF-RESPECT

He that respects himself is safe from others; he wears a coat of mail that none can pierce.
*Henry W. Longfellow*

## SELF-SACRIFICE

Greater love hath no man than this, that a man lay down his life for his friends.
*John 15:13*

Present your bodies a living sacrifice, holy, acceptable unto God.
*Romans 12:1*

## SELFISHNESS

Most men live on the cafeteria plan—self-service only.

Everyone is eloquent in his own cause.
*Latin proverb*

## SENSITIVITY

Exaggerated sensitiveness is an expression of the feeling of inferiority.
*Alfred Adler*

## SENSUALITY

If sensuality were happiness, beasts were happier than men; but human felicity is lodged in the soul, not in the flesh.
*Seneca*

## SERENITY

After a storm comes a calm.

## SERVANT

He that is greatest among you shall be your servant.
*Matthew 23:11*

A servant is known by his master's absence.

Few men have been admired by their servants.
*Michel de Montaigne*

## SERVICE

He profits most who serves best.
*Arthur F. Sheldon*

## SHAME

Shame lasts longer than poverty.
*Dutch proverb*

Who has no shame before men, has no fear of God.
*Yiddish proverb*

## SHEEP

The sheep has no choice when in the jaws of the wolf.
*Chinese proverb*

## SHIPS

Ships that pass in the night.
*Henry W. Longfellow*

## SHIPWRECK

He who will not be ruled by the rudder must be ruled by the rock.

Each man makes his own shipwreck.
*Latin proverb*

## SHOPPING CART

The most expensive vehicle to operate, per mile, is the shopping cart.

## SHORTCOMINGS

I wish I were honest enough to admit all my shortcomings:
—brilliant enough to accept flattery without it making me arrogant;
—tall enough to tower above deceit;
—strong enough to treasure love;
—brave enough to welcome criticism;
—compassionate enough to understand human frailties;
—wise enough to recognize my mistakes;

—humble enough to appreciate greatness;
—staunch enough to stand by my friends;
—human enough to be thoughtful of my neighbor;
—and righteous enough to be devoted to the love of God.
*Gordon H. Taggart*

## SICKNESS

No one else feels worse than the man who gets sick on his day off.

Be not slow to visit the sick.

It is much more important to know what sort of a patient has a disease than what sort of a disease a patient has.
*William Osler*

Sickness is every man's master.
*Danish proverb*

How sickness enlarges the dimensions of a man's self to himself.
*Charles Lamb*

In time of sickness the soul collects itself anew.
*Latin proverb*

Sickness shows us what we are.
*Latin proverb*

## SIGHT

One man does not see everything.
*Greek proverb*

Seeing is believing.
*Latin proverb*

## SILENCE

Keep quiet and people will think you a philosopher.
*Latin proverb*

He that keepeth his mouth keepeth his life: but he that openeth wide his lips shall have destruction.
*Proverbs 13:3*

I regret often that I have spoken; never that I have been silent.
*Publilius Syrus*

He has the gift of quiet.
*John Le Carré*

Silence is the most perfect expression of scorn.
*George Bernard Shaw*

Silence propagates itself, and the longer talk has been
suspended, the more difficult it is to find anything to say.
*Samuel Johnson*

Better to remain silent and be thought a fool, than to speak
out and remove all doubt.
*Abraham Lincoln*

Even silence may be eloquent.

He is not a fool who knows when to hold his tongue.

Little said is soonest mended.

Silence seldom hurts.

When you have nothing to say, say nothing.

Speech is silver, silence is golden.
*French proverb*

If a word be worth one shekel, silence is worth two.
*Hebrew proverb*

Silence is also speech.
*Yiddish proverb*

Silence is the ultimate weapon of power.
*Charles de Gaulle*

He had occasional flashes of silence that made his conversation
perfectly delightful.
*Sydney Smith*

## SILLINESS

A silly remark can be made in Latin as well as in Spanish.
*Miguel de Cervantes*

## SIN

Two things never live up to their advertising claims: the circus and sin.

He that is without sin among you, let him first cast a stone at her.
*John 8:7*

Be sure your sin will find you out.
*Numbers 32:23*

The wages of sin is death.
*Romans 6:23*

## SLANDER

A slander is like a hornet; if you cannot kill it dead the first blow, better not strike at it.
*H. W. Shaw*

If slander be a snake, it is a winged one—it flies as well as creeps.
*D. W. Jerrold*

Slander slays three persons: the speaker, the spoken to, and the spoken of.
*Hebrew proverb*

No character, however upright, is a match for constantly reiterated attacks, however false.
*Alexander Hamilton*

Slander-mongers and those who listen to slander, if I had my way, would all be strung up, the talkers by the tongue, the listeners by the ears.
*Plautus*

Character assassination is at once easier and surer than physical assault; and it involves far less risk for the assassin. It leaves him free to commit the same deed over and over again, and may, indeed, win him the honors of a hero even in the country of his victims.
*Alan Barth*

To murder character is as truly a crime as to murder the body; the tongue of the slanderer is brother to the dagger of the assassin.
*Tryon Edwards*

The worthiest people are the most injured by slander, as is the best fruit which the birds have been pecking at.
*Jonathan Swift*

Have patience awhile; slanders are not long-lived. Truth is the child of time; ere long she shall appear to vindicate thee.
*Immanuel Kant*

## SLANG

Slang is a language that rolls up its sleeves, spits on its hands and goes to work.
*Carl Sandburg*

## SLEEP

Sleeping at the wheel is a good way to keep from growing old.

Yet a little sleep, a little slumber, a little folding of the hands to sleep . . .
*Proverbs 6:10*

The sleep of a labouring man is sweet.
*Ecclesiastes 5:12*

A man is not always asleep when his eyes are shut.

One hour's sleep before midnight is worth three afterwards.

Sleep . . . knits up the ravell'd sleeve of care.
*William Shakespeare*

I never sleep comfortably except when I am at sermon.
*Francois Rabelais*

Five hours of sleep a traveler, seven a scholar, eight a merchant, and eleven every knave.
*Italian proverb*

Sleep is the best cure for waking troubles.
*Spanish proverb*

Fatigue is the best pillow.
*Benjamin Franklin*

## SMALL TOWN

A small town is where the newspaper prints the crossword puzzle on the front page.

## SMILE

One may smile, and smile, and be a villain.
*William Shakespeare*

A smile is a light in the window of a face which shows that the heart is at home.

## SMOKING

As ye smoke, so shall ye reek.

## SNAKE

When you see a snake, never mind where he came from.

## SNOBBERY

Laughter would be bereaved if snobbery died.
*Peter Ustinov*

## SNORE

Smile and the world smiles with you; snore and you sleep alone.

## SNOW

Snow is beautiful—when you're watching the other fellow shovel it.

## SOCIAL SECURITY

Suspenders are the oldest form of social security.

## SOLDIER

An army, like a serpent, travels on its belly.
*Frederick the Great*

## SOLEMNITY

Nothing in the world annoys a man more than not being taken seriously.
*Palacio Valdes*

## SOLITUDE

One can acquire everything in solitude but character.
*Stendhal*

Man cannot long survive without air, water, and sleep. Next in importance comes food. And close on its heels, solitude.
*Thomas Szasz*

Solitude is the profoundest fact of the human condition. Man is the only being who knows he is alone.
*Octavio Paz*

Pray that your loneliness may spur you into finding something to live for, great enough to die for.
*Dag Hammarskjold*

## SOLUTION

There is always an easy solution to every human problem—neat, plausible, and wrong.
*H. L. Mencken*

## SON

A wise son maketh a glad father: but a foolish son is the heaviness of his mother.
*Proverbs 10:1*

## SONG

Our sweetest songs are those that tell of saddest thought.
*Percy B. Shelley*

What will a child learn sooner than a song?

Men, when alone, lighten their labor by song, however rude.
*Latin proverb*

He who sings scares away his woes.
*Spanish proverb*

These days, what isn't worth saying is sung.
*Pierre de Beaumarchais*

## SORROW

Sorrows are like thunderclouds—in the distance they look
black, over our heads scarcely gray.
*Jean Paul Richter*

There can be no rainbow without a cloud and a storm.
*J. H. Vincent*

A moment of time may make us unhappy forever.
*John Gay*

In extreme youth, in our most humiliating sorrow, we think
we are alone. When we are older we find that others have
suffered too.
*Suzanne Moarny*

When sorrows come, they come not as single spies, but in
battalions!
*William Shakespeare*

A day of sorrow is longer than a month of joy.
*Chinese proverb*

Earth has no sorrow that Heaven cannot heal.
*Thomas Moore*

Sorrow will pay no debt.

Into each life some rain must fall.
*Henry W. Longfellow*

Sorrow makes men sincere.
*Henry Ward Beecher*

The empty vessel makes the greatest sound.
*William Shakespeare*

## SOUL

For what shall it profit a man, if he shall gain the whole world,
and lose his own soul?
*Mark 8:36*

God help my poor soul.
*Edgar Allan Poe*

Be careless in your dress if you must, but keep a tidy soul.
*Mark Twain*

There is nothing the body suffers that the soul may not profit by.

## SOW
He that sows thistles shall reap prickles.

## SPARK
A little spark kindles a great fire.
*Italian proverb*

## SPEAKERS
Too many after-dinner speakers are merely after dinner.

The recipe for a good speech includes some shortening.

A speech is like a wheel—the longer the spoke, the greater the tire.

Some people know very little, but they know it fluently.

If your mind goes blank—be sure to turn off the sound.

## SPECIALIST
A specialist is a doctor who diagnoses your case by feeling your wallet.

A specialist is a doctor whose patients can only be ill during office hours.

## SPEECH
Blessed is the man who, having nothing to say, abstains from giving us wordy evidence of the fact.
*George Eliot*

It is terrible to speak well and be wrong.
*Sophocles*

Once you get people laughing, they're listening and you can tell them almost anything.
*Herbert Gardner*

When a man gets talking about himself, he seldom fails to be eloquent and often reaches the sublime.
*Josh Billings*

Oratory: the art of making deep noises from the chest that sound like important messages from the brain.
*H. I. Phillips*

First learn the meaning of what you say, and then speak.
*Epictetus*

When a man is asked to make a speech, the first thing he has to decide is what to say.
*Gerald Ford*

The whale only gets harpooned when he spouts.
*Henry Lea Hillman*

Why don't the feller who says, "I'm not a speechmaker," let it go at that instead o' givin' a demonstration?
*Frank M. Hubbard*

Let your speech be always with grace, seasoned with salt.
*Colossians 4:6*

Every man has a right to utter what he thinks truth, and every other man has a right to knock him down for it.
*Samuel Johnson*

Woe unto you, when all men shall speak well of you!
*Luke 6:26*

A soft answer turneth away wrath.
*Proverbs 15:1*

Remember, every time you open your mouth to talk, your mind walks out and parades up and down the words.
*Edwin H. Stuart*

First think, and then speak.

He cannot speak well that cannot hold his tongue.

He that speaks much is much mistaken.

Hear much, speak little.

Speaking without thinking is shooting without aiming.

Teach your child to hold his tongue; he'll learn fast enough to speak.

They talk most who have the least to say.

Much speaking and lying are cousins.
*German proverb*

To speak much is one thing, to speak well, another.
*Greek proverb*

It is easy for men to say one thing and think another.
*Latin proverb*

Speech both conceals and reveals the thoughts of men.
*Latin proverb*

## SPIRIT

He that is slow to anger is better than the mighty; and he that ruleth his spirit than he that taketh a city.
*Proverbs 16:32*

A wounded spirit who can bear?
*Proverbs 18:14*

There are only two forces in the world, the sword and the spirit. In the long run the sword will always be conquered by the spirit.
*Napoleon Bonaparte*

## SPORTS

Jogging is very beneficial. It's good for your legs and your feet. It's also very good for the ground. It makes it feel needed.
*Charles M. Schulz*

Becoming number one is easier than remaining number one.
*Bill Bradley*

## SPRING
In the spring a young man's fancy lightly turns to thoughts of love.
*Alfred, Lord Tennyson*

## STEAL
He that will steal a pin will steal an ox.

## STILL
Beware of still water, a still dog, and a still enemy.
*Yiddish proverb*

## STOCK
I won some stock in a company that pays quarterly dividends. Every three months they send me a quarter.

## STOCKBROKER
A stockbroker is a man who is always ready to back his judgment with your last dollar.

## STOCKS
Many an innocent lamb is drowned in a stock pool.

A stock market investor is someone who is alert, informed, attuned to the economic heartbeat of America, and cries a lot.

I've been burned in the stock market by picking up a hot tip.

A friend in need is a friend who has been playing the stock market.

People who play the market are often led astray by false profits.

The only difference between the current stock market and the Titanic is that the Titanic had a band.

I'll never understand the stock market. Some of my stocks just went from the financial page to the comics.

## STOMACH
The stomach is easier filled than the eye.
*German proverb*

The way to a man's heart is through his stomach.
*Spanish proverb*

## STORM
Any port in a storm.

## STORYTELLING
A good tale ill told is marred in the telling.

A tale never loses in the telling.

## STRAW
The last straw breaks the camel's back.

## STRENGTH
My strength is made perfect in weakness.
*2 Corinthians 12:9*

They that wait upon the LORD shall renew their strength.
*Isaiah 40:31*

An oak is not felled at one stroke.

## STUDY
If I had only three years to serve the Lord, I would spend two of them studying and preparing.
*Donald Grey Barnhouse*

## SUBJECTIVITY
The fly sat upon the axle-tree of the chariot-wheel and said, What a dust do I raise!
*Francis Bacon*

## SUBMISSION
If two men ride on a horse, one must ride behind.

## SUCCESS
Success gives some people big heads, and others big headaches.

Women are rarely as successful as men—they have no wives to advise them.

Success is relative. The more success, the more relatives.

Before success comes in any man's life, he is sure to meet with much temporary defeat, and, perhaps, some failure. When defeat overtakes a man, the easiest and most logical thing to do is to quit. That is exactly what the majority of men do.
*Napoleon Hill*

Better to love God and die unknown than to love the world and be a hero; better to be content with poverty than to die a slave to wealth; better to have taken some risks and lost than to have done nothing and succeeded at it; better to have lost some battles than to have retreated from the war; better to have failed when serving God than to have succeeded when serving the devil. What a tragedy to climb the ladder of success only to discover that the ladder was leaning against the wrong wall.
*Erwin W. Lutzer*

Of course there is no formula for success except, perhaps, an unconditional acceptance of life and what it brings.
*Arthur Rubinstein*

Success has ruined many a man.
*Benjamin Franklin*

Elbow grease is still the best lubricant for success.
*Anonymous*

Never contend with a man who has nothing to lose.
*Baltasar Gracian*

There is always something about your success that displeases even your best friends.
*Oscar Wilde*

Success is a ladder which cannot be climbed with your hands in your pockets.

Success has many friends.
*Greek proverb*

We can come to look upon the deaths of our enemies with as much regret as we feel for those of our friends, namely, when we miss their existence as witnesses to our success.
*Arthur Schopenhauer*

For a hundred that can bear adversity there is hardly one that can bear prosperity.
*Thomas Carlyle*

To climb steep hills requires slow pace at first.
*William Shakespeare*

## SUFFERING

There is one psychological peculiarity in the human being that always strikes one: to shun even the slightest signs of trouble on the outer edge of your existence at times of well-being . . . to try not to know about the sufferings of others and your own or one's own future sufferings, to yield in many situations, even important spiritual and central ones—as long as it prolongs one's well-being.
*Alexander Solzhenitsyn*

The truth that many people never understand, until it is too late, is that the more you try to avoid suffering the more you suffer because smaller and more insignificant things begin to torture you in proportion to your fear of being hurt.
*Thomas Merton*

## SUNTAN

When it comes to getting a suntan, ignorance is blister.

## SUPERIORITY

Superiority is always detested.
*Baltasar Gracian*

## SURVIVAL

To survive it is often necessary to fight, and to fight you have to dirty yourself.
*George Orwell*

Once one determines that he or she has a mission in life, that it's not going to be accomplished without a great deal of pain, and that the rewards in the end may not outweigh the pain— if you recognize historically that always happens, then when it comes, you survive it.
*Richard Nixon*

## SUSPICION

The less we know the more we suspect.
*H. W. Shaw*

Suspicion may be no fault, but showing it may be a great one.

What loneliness is more lonely than distrust?
*George Eliot*

A wise man will keep his suspicions muzzled, but he will keep them awake.
*Marquess of Halifax*

## SWINE

You cannot make a satin purse of a sow's ear.

Feed a pig and you'll have a hog.

## SYMPATHY

Sympathy is what one usually gives to a friend or relative when he doesn't want to lend him money.

Rejoice with them that do rejoice, and weep with them that weep.
*Romans 12:15*

No one really understands the grief or joy of another.
*Franz Schubert*

People in distress never think that you feel enough.

## SYSTEM

A place for everything and everything in its place.

TACT—TYRANNY

# TACT

Social tact is making your company feel at home, even though you wish they were.

Tact is the ability to arrive at conclusions without expressing them.

Tact is giving a person a shot in the arm without letting him feel the needle.

Tact is the ability to shut your mouth before someone else does.

Tact is the ability to describe others as they see themselves.
*Abraham Lincoln*

Don't flatter yourself that friendship authorizes you to say disagreeable things to your intimates. The nearer you come into relation with a person, the more necessary do tact and courtesy become.
*Oliver Wendell Holmes*

# TALK

I thought talk was cheap until I saw our telephone bill.

If you want your wife to listen to you, talk to another woman.

Talk does not cook rice.
*Chinese proverb*

When I can't talk sense, I talk metaphor.
*John Philpot Curran*

He who talks much is sometimes right.
*Spanish proverb*

Don't talk about yourself; it will be done when you leave.
*Addison Mitzner*

Two great talkers will not travel far together.
*Spanish proverb*

Some people would say more if they talked less.

I don't like people to talk while I'm interrupting.

Another of life's problems is how to keep ignorant people from talking.

## TAX COLLECTOR

The tax collector is a man looking for untold wealth.

## TAX LOOPHOLES

Tax loopholes are like parking spaces—they all seem to disappear by the time you get there.

## TAXES

The Eiffel Tower is the Empire State Building after taxes.
*Anonymous*

Next to being shot at and missed, nothing is quite as satisfying as an income tax refund.
*F. J. Raymond*

There went out a decree from Caesar Augustus, that all the world should be taxed. . . . And all went to be taxed, every one into his own city.
*Luke 2:1-3*

Render therefore unto Caesar the things which are Caesar's; and unto God the things that are God's.
*Matthew 22:21*

A fine is a tax you pay for doing wrong, and a tax is a fine you pay for doing all right.

Everybody should pay his income tax with a smile. I tried it, but they wanted cash.

I went to Washington and visited the Tax Department. I just wanted to see the people I'm working for.

With my latest raise, I can now afford to pay last year's taxes.

I'm putting all my money in taxes—it is the only thing sure to go up.

Patrick Henry should come back to see what taxation with representation is like.

When a Congressman says he's for a tax cut—it simply means he wants his cut of your taxes.

There's only one thing to be said about the wages of sin. It's about the only wage the government doesn't tax.

A taxpayer is a person who has the government on his payroll.

## TEACHING

A professor is one who talks in someone else's sleep.
*W. H. Auden*

Old teachers never die, they just grade away.

He who can, does. He who cannot, teaches.
*George Bernard Shaw*

A teacher affects eternity; he can never tell where his influence stops.
*Henry Adams*

Thoroughly to teach another is the best way to learn for yourself.
*Tryon Edwards*

The secret of teaching is to appear to have known all your life what you learned this afternoon.
*Anonymous*

True teaching, then, is not that which gives knowledge, but that which stimulates pupils to gain it.
*Milton Gregory*

You cannot teach a man anything; you can only help him to find it within himself.
*Galileo*

## TEAMWORK

No member of a crew is praised for the rugged individuality of his rowing.
*Ralph Waldo Emerson*

Light is the task where many share the toil.
*Homer*

A major reason capable people fail to advance is that they don't work well with their colleagues.
*Lee Iacocca*

## TEARS

A small tear relieves a great sorrow.

In youth, one has tears without grief; in age, grief without tears.
*French proverb*

Repentant tears wash out the stain of guilt.
*Latin proverb*

## TECHNOLOGY

To err is human, but to really foul things up requires a computer.
*Anonymous*

## TEENAGER

Teenagers are always ready to give adults the full benefit of their inexperience.

Teenagers complain that there's nothing to do and then stay out all night getting it done.

Teenagers express a burning desire to be different by dressing exactly alike.

## TEETH

I have so much gold in my teeth, I have to sleep with my head in a safe.

## TELEVISION

A good TV mystery is one where it's hard to detect the sponsor.

TV has made dull conversationalists of us all—it even has people to talk about the weather for us.

Television is an invention that permits you to be entertained in your living room by people you wouldn't have in your home.
*David Frost*

## TEMPTATION

There hath no temptation taken you but such as is common to man: but God is faithful, who will not suffer you to be tempted above that ye are able; but will with the temptation also make a way to escape, that ye may be able to bear it.
*1 Corinthians 10:13*

Temptation rarely comes in working hours. It is in their leisure time that men are made or marred.
*W. M. Taylor*

Things forbidden have a secret charm.
*Tacitus*

Never give in, never give in, never, never, never, never—in nothing great or small, large or petty—never give in except to convictions of honour and good sense.
*Winston Churchill*

Saintliness is also a temptation.
*Jean Anouilh*

An open door may tempt a saint.

Blessed is the man that endureth temptation.
*James 1:12*

I can resist everything except temptation.
*Oscar Wilde*

It is easier to stay out than get out.
*Mark Twain*

## THANKSGIVING

We are having the usual thing for our Thanksgiving dinner: relatives.

## THEATER

The show was so bad people were lined up to get out of the theater.

All the movies used to be "colossal." Now they're all "frank." I think I liked "colossal" better.
*Beryl Pfizer*

When the audience knows you know better, it's satire, but when they think you can't do any better, it's corn.
*Spike Jones*

## THEOLOGY
Division has done more to hide Christ from the view of all men than all the infidelity that has ever been spoken.
*George MacDonald*

## THERAPIST
In California everyone goes to a therapist, is a therapist, or is a therapist going to a therapist.
*Truman Capote*

## THIEF
A thief knows a thief as a wolf knows a wolf.

## THINKING
We only think when we are confronted with a problem.
*John Dewey*

When a man knows he is to be hanged in a fortnight, it concentrates his mind wonderfully.
*Samuel Johnson*

And which of you with taking thought can add to his stature one cubit?
*Luke 12:25*

Thinking is the hardest work there is, which is the probable reason why so few engage in it.
*Henry Ford Sr.*

As he thinketh in his heart, so is he.
*Proverbs 23:7*

Curiosity is, in great and generous minds, the first passion and the last.
*Samuel Johnson*

A thought is often original, though you have uttered it a hundred times.
*Oliver Wendell Holmes*

Any man may make a mistake; none but a fool will stick to it. Second thoughts are best, as the proverb says.
*Cicero*

Great thoughts reduced to practice become great acts.
*William Hazlitt*

They are never alone that are accompanied with noble thoughts.
*Philip Sidney*

A thought may take a man prisoner.

Think much, speak little, and write less.
*French proverb*

Men suffer from thinking more than from anything else.
*Leo Tolstoy*

You are today where your thoughts have brought you; you will be tomorrow where your thoughts take you.
*James Allen*

## THIRST

I am the bread of life: he that cometh to me shall never hunger; and he that believeth on me shall never thirst.
*John 6:35*

## TIME

You can't make footprints in the sands of time sitting down.

To every thing there is a season, and a time to every purpose under the heaven.
*Ecclesiastes 3:1*

Time is a great teacher, but unfortunately it kills all its pupils.
*Hector Berlioz*

Time gives good advice.
*Maltese proverb*

Time wounds all heels.
*Jane Ace*

Dost thou love life? Then do not squander time, for that's the stuff life is made of.
*Benjamin Franklin*

Time and tide wait for no man.

All the treasures of earth cannot bring back one lost moment.
*French proverb*

Time is money.
*Greek proverb*

The happier the time, the more quickly it passes.
*Latin proverb*

Time is the wisest of all counselors.
*Plutarch*

## TIRED

When you feel dog-tired at night, it may be because you've growled all day long.

Tired folks are quarrelsome.
*French proverb*

## TOBACCO

I have never smoked in my life and look forward to a time when the world will look back in amazement and disgust to a practice so unnatural and offensive.
*George Bernard Shaw*

## TODAY

We are here today and gone tomorrow.
*Anonymous*

One today is worth two tomorrows.
*Benjamin Franklin*

## TOIL

He who toils with pain will eat with pleasure.
*Chinese proverb*

## TOLERANCE

Why beholdest thou the mote that is in thy brother's eye, but considerest not the beam that is in thine own eye?
*Matthew 7:3*

Judge not, and ye shall not be judged: condemn not, and ye shall not be condemned: forgive, and ye shall be forgiven.
*Luke 6:37*

## TOMORROW

No one has ever seen tomorrow.

Tomorrow, tomorrow, not today,
Hear the lazy people say.
*German proverb*

## TONGUE

Keep thy tongue from evil, and thy lips from speaking guile.
*Psalm 34:13*

The tongue can no man tame; it is an unruly evil.
*James 3:8*

A slip of the foot may be soon recovered; but that of the tongue, perhaps never.

Let not your tongue cut your throat.

There is no venom to that of the tongue.

The tongue is a wild beast; once let it loose, it is difficult to chain.
*Latin proverb*

## TORTURE

The healthy man does not torture others—generally it is the tortured who turn into torturers.
*Carl Jung*

## TOUPEE

Today's toupees really fool people, but only those people who wear them.

## TRAINING

A bustling mother makes a slothful daughter.

A man can seldom—very, very, seldom—fight a winning fight against his training: the odds are too heavy.
*Mark Twain*

## TRAVEL

Travel brings out anything in a man—especially sea travel.

Travel broadens people—it also flattens them.

## TREE

The tree is known by its fruit.
*Matthew 12:33*

The highest tree hath the greatest fall.

## TRICK

There are tricks in every trade.

## TRIFLE

Little drops of water, little grains of sand,
Make the mighty ocean and the pleasant land.
*J. F. Carney*

A trifle consoles us because a trifle upsets us.
*Blaise Pascal*

For the want of a nail the shoe was lost,
For the want of a shoe the horse was lost,
For the want of a horse the rider was lost,
For the want of a rider the battle was lost,
For the want of a battle the kingdom was lost,
And all for the want of a horse-shoe nail.
*Benjamin Franklin*

## TROUBLE

Troubles are a lot like babies—they grow larger if you nurse them.

The trouble with trouble is that it always starts out like fun.

Every heart hath its own ache.

The true way to soften one's troubles is to solace those of others.
*Mme. de Maintenon*

He that seeks trouble always finds it.
*English proverb*

Don't cross the bridge till you get to it.

In trouble to be troubled is to have your trouble doubled.

Never meet trouble halfway.

Never trouble trouble till trouble troubles you.

The troubles hardest to bear are those that never come.

Forgetting trouble is the way to cure it.
*Latin proverb*

The best place to put your troubles is in your pocket—the one with a hole in it.

If I had a formula for bypassing trouble, I wouldn't pass it around. Wouldn't be doing anybody a favour. Trouble creates a capacity to handle it. I don't say embrace trouble. That's as bad as treating it as an enemy. But I do say, meet it as a friend, for you'll see a lot of it and had better be on speaking terms with it.
*Oliver Wendell Holmes Jr.*

## TRUST

To be trusted is a greater compliment than to be loved.
*George MacDonald*

In God we trust; all others cash.
*American proverb*

I will trust him no farther than I can throw a millstone.

Who mistrusts most should be trusted least.
*Greek proverb*

It is equally an error to trust all men or no man.
*Latin proverb*

## TRUTH

The trouble with stretching the truth is that it's apt to snap back.

My way of joking is to tell the truth. It's the funniest joke in the world.
*George Bernard Shaw*

Truth is such a rare thing, it is delightful to tell it.
*Emily Dickinson*

A man had rather have a hundred lies told of him, than one truth which he does not wish should be told.
*Samuel Johnson*

A half truth, like half a brick, is always more forcible as an argument than a whole one. It carries better.
*Stephen Leacock*

Every truth has two faces, every rule two surfaces, every precept two applications.
*Joseph Joubert*

What probably distorts everything in life is that one is convinced that one is speaking the truth because one says what one thinks.
*Sacha Guitry*

Seldom any splendid story is wholly true.
*Samuel Johnson*

The truth is too simple: one must always get there by a complicated route.

A striking expression, with the aid of a small amount of truth, can surprise us into accepting a falsehood.
*Marquis de Vauvenargues*

And ye shall know the truth, and the truth shall make you free.
*John 8:32*

The man who speaks the truth is always at ease.
*Persian proverb*

Truth for him was a moving target; he never aimed for the bull and rarely pierced the outer ring.
*Hugh Cudlipp*

Between whom there is hearty truth, there is love.
*Henry David Thoreau*

If you speak the truth have a foot in the stirrup.
*Turkish proverb*

There's such a thing as moderation, even in telling the truth.
*Vera Johnson*

A lie travels round the world while Truth is putting on her boots.

All truths are not to be told.

Half the truth is often a great lie.

Truth is . . . stranger than fiction.
*Lord Byron*

Truth is the anvil which has worn out many a hammer.

Truth needs no memory.

When in doubt, tell the truth.
*Mark Twain*

We know the truth not only by the reason but also by the heart.
*Blaise Pascal*

The truth is always the strongest argument.
*Greek proverb*

Truth is heavy; few therefore can bear it.
*Hebrew proverb*

He who would speak the truth must keep a sharp lookout.
*Italian proverb*

Everyone loves the truth, but not everyone tells it.
*Yiddish proverb*

Men occasionally stumble over the truth, but most of them pick themselves up and hurry off as if nothing happened.
*Winston Churchill*

It is easier to perceive error than to find truth, for the former lies on the surface and is easily seen, while the latter lies in the depth, where few are willing to search for it.
*Johann Goethe*

Craft must have clothes, but truth loves to go naked.
*Thomas Fuller*

He who tells the truth saves himself the trouble of swearing.
*Yiddish proverb*

## TURN
Turn about is fair play.

## TWO

Two eyes can see more than one.

Two heads are better than one.

Two watermelons cannot be held under one arm.
*Turkish proverb*

## TYRANNY

Any excuse will serve a tyrant.
*Aesop*

Dictators ride to and fro on tigers from which they dare not dismount.
*Hindustani proverb*

Tyranny is always better organized than freedom.
*Charles Peguy*

The face of tyranny is always mild at first.
*Jean Racine*

The closed door and the sealed lips are prerequisites to tyranny.
*Frank L. Stanton*

# U

UNDERSTANDING—UNITY

## UNDERSTANDING
One learns people through the heart, not the eyes or the intellect.
*Mark Twain*

Nothing can be loved or hated unless it is first known.
*Leonardo da Vinci*

## UNEMPLOYMENT
Better to wear out shoes than sheets.
*English proverb*

## UNHAPPINESS
The sole cause of man's unhappiness is that he does not know how to stay quietly in his room.
*Blaise Pascal*

## UNITY
United we stand, divided we fall.
*Aesop*

No man can serve two masters.
*Matthew 6:24*

If a house be divided against itself, that house cannot stand.
*Mark 3:25*

A threefold cord is not quickly broken.
*Ecclesiastes 4:12*

Behold, how good and how pleasant it is for brethren to dwell together in unity!
*Psalm 133:1*

We must all hang together, or we shall all hang separately.
*Benjamin Franklin*

Weak things united become strong.

If a link is broken, the whole chain breaks.
*Yiddish proverb*

# V

VACATION—VOW

## VACATION

When you start to look like your passport photo—you know you need a vacation.

No man needs a vacation so much as the man who has just had one.
*Elbert Hubbard*

A vacation is over when you begin to yearn for your work.
*Morris Fishbein*

## VALLEY

He that stays in the valley shall never get over the hill.

## VALOR

The better part of valor is discretion.

## VALUES

You must lose a fly to catch a trout.
*George Herbert*

It's not hard to make decisions when you know what your values are.
*Roy Disney*

Neither cast ye your pearls before swine, lest they trample them under their feet, and turn again and rend you.
*Matthew 7:6*

What costs little is valued less.
*Miguel de Cervantes*

I conceive that the great part of the miseries of mankind are brought upon them by false estimates they have made of the value of things.
*Benjamin Franklin*

## VANITY

Vanity of vanities . . . all is vanity.
*Ecclesiastes 1:2*

"Your feet are crooked, your hair is good for nothing," said the pig to the horse.
*Russian proverb*

## VARIETY

With me a change of trouble is as good as a vacation.
*William Lloyd George*

Variety is the mother of enjoyment.

Variety is the spice of life.

Variety's the very spice of life, that gives it all its flavor.
*William Cowper*

## VENGEANCE

The best manner of avenging ourselves is by not resembling him who has injured us.
*Jane Porter*

## VENTURE

Nothing ventured, nothing have.

## VICE

If you don't want anyone to know it, don't do it.
*Chinese proverb*

Vices are learned without a master.

Great abilities produce great vices as well as virtues.
*Greek proverb*

To flee vice is the beginning of virtue.
*Latin proverb*

Vice is nourished by concealment.
*Latin proverb*

Vices creep into our hearts under the name of virtues.
*Latin proverb*

After one vice a greater follows.
*Spanish proverb*

## VICTORY

There are some defeats more triumphant than victories.
*Michel de Montaigne*

Victories that are easy are cheap. Those only are worth having which come as the result of hard fighting.
*Henry Ward Beecher*

It is fatal to enter any war without the will to win it.
*General Douglas MacArthur*

## VIRTUE
Kindness affects more than severity.
*Aesop*

Righteousness exalteth a nation.
*Proverbs 14:34*

Strait is the gate, and narrow is the way, which leadeth unto life, and few there be that find it.
*Matthew 7:14*

Virtue is not left to stand alone.
*Chinese proverb*

## VISION
The farther backward you can look, the farther forward you are likely to see.
*Winston Churchill*

Vision is the art of seeing things invisible.
*Jonathan Swift*

Where there is no vision, the people perish.
*Proverbs 29:18*

## VISIT
Friendship increases by visiting friends, but by visiting seldom.

If you'd lose a troublesome visitor, lend him money.

Santa Claus has the right idea; visit people once a year.
*Victor Borge*

## VOW
Vows are made in storms and forgotten in calms.

# W

WAGES—WRONG

## WAGES

Be content with your wages.
*Luke 3:14*

## WAIT

They also serve who only stand and wait.
*John Milton*

When you do not know what to do—wait.

## WALL

A white wall is the fool's paper.
*Italian proverb*

## WALL STREET

The bulls and bears aren't dangerous on Wall Street—it's the bum steers.

You must look on the positive side of Wall Street. Like the sound, secure investments of today are the tax losses of tomorrow.

## WANT

The more one has, the more one wants.

Bad is want which is born of plenty.
*Latin proverb*

## WAR

War hath no fury like a noncombatant.
*C. E. Montague*

War does not determine who is right—only who is left.
*Anonymous*

The war has already almost destroyed that nation. . . . I have seen, I guess, as much blood and disaster as any living man, and it just turned my stomach the last time I was there. After I looked at that wreckage and those thousands of women and children and everything, I vomited.
*General Douglas MacArthur*

War is the child of pride.

As long as there are sovereign nations possessing great power, war is inevitable.
*Albert Einstein*

For a war to be just, three things are necessary—public authority, just cause, right motive.
*St. Thomas Aquinas*

## WASTE
Willful waste brings woeful want.

Short as life is, we make it still shorter by the careless waste of time.
*Victor Hugo*

I wish I could stand on a busy street corner, hat in hand, and beg people to throw me all their wasted hours.
*Bernard Berenson*

## WATER
The water that comes from the same spring cannot be fresh and stale both.

## WEALTH
I'm opposed to millionaires, but it would be dangerous to offer me the position.
*Mark Twain*

Be rich in good works.
*1 Timothy 6:18*

All wealth is the product of labor.
*John Locke*

Riches certainly make themselves wings.
*Proverbs 23:5*

Great wealth and content seldom live together.

## WEEDS
Weeds never die.
*German proverb*

## WEEP

Better the cottage where one is merry than the palace where one weeps.
*Chinese proverb*

Weeping makes the heart grow lighter.
*Yiddish proverb*

## WELCOME

Do not outstay your welcome.

He who brings is welcome.
*German proverb*

He who comes seldom is welcome.
*Italian proverb*

## WELL

Don't throw a stone into a well from which you have drunk.
*Yiddish proverb*

## WELL-INFORMED

It's easy to spot a well-informed man—his views coincide with yours.

## WHEEL

The wheel that does the squeaking is the one that gets the grease.

The worst wheel of the cart makes the most noise.

## WHISPER

What is whispered in your ear is often heard a hundred miles off.
*Chinese proverb*

## WICKED

There may be no rest for the wicked, but there is often arrest.

Let the wicked forsake his way.
*Isaiah 55:7*

There is no peace . . . unto the wicked.
*Isaiah 48:22*

No man ever became wicked all at once.
*Latin proverb*

## WIFE

My wife has a whim of iron.

Try praising your wife, even if at first it frightens her.

A prudent wife is from the LORD.
*Proverbs 19:14*

Whoso findeth a wife findeth a good thing.
*Proverbs 18:22*

Of all the home remedies, a good wife is best.
*Kin Hubbard*

A wife is a gift bestowed upon man to reconcile him to the loss of paradise.
*Johann Goethe*

## WILL

Where there's a will, there's a way.

People do not lack strength; they lack will.
*Victor Hugo*

Strength does not come from physical capacity. It comes from an indomitable will.
*Mahatma Gandhi*

## WINE

There is a devil in every berry of the grape.
*The Koran*

Wine is a mocker, strong drink is raging.
*Proverbs 20:1*

## WINNING

The most difficult part of getting to the top of the ladder is getting through the crowd at the bottom.
*Arch Ward*

## WISDOM

The price of wisdom is above rubies.
*Job 28:18*

Through wisdom a house is built, and by understanding it is established.
*Proverbs 24:3 (NKJV)*

Wisdom is only a comparative quality, it will not bear a single definition.
*Marquess of Halifax*

In much wisdom is much grief: and he that increaseth knowledge increaseth sorrow.
*Ecclesiastes 1:18*

The wisdom of this world is foolishness with God.
*1 Corinthians 3:19*

A man should never be ashamed to own that he has been in the wrong, which is but saying, in other words, that he is wiser today than he was yesterday.
*Jonathan Swift*

The fear of the LORD is the beginning of wisdom.
*Psalm 111:10*

## WISE

Everybody is wise after the thing has happened.
*French proverb*

The words of the wise are as goads.
*Ecclesiastes 12:11*

The wise man would rather see men needing him than thanking him.
*Baltasar Gracian*

Great men are not always wise.
*Job 32:9*

It is not wise to be wiser than is necessary.
*Philippe Quinault*

A wise man's question contains half the answer.
*Solomon Ibn Gabirol*

A wise man sees as much as he ought, not as much as he can.
*Michel de Montaigne*

Among mortals second thoughts are wisest.
*Euripides*

If you run through the streets, saying you imitate a lunatic, you are in fact a lunatic. If you kill a man, saying you imitate a criminal, you are a criminal yourself. A man who studies wisdom, even insincerely, should be called wise.
*Yoshida Kenko*

It is more easy to be wise for others than for ourselves.
*La Rochefoucauld*

It is easy to be wise after the event.

## WISH

If wishes were horses, beggars might ride.
*English proverb*

If a man could half his wishes he would double his Troubles.
*Benjamin Franklin*

When wishing won't work, work.

Wishes won't wash dishes.

If things are not as you wish, wish them as they are.
*Yiddish proverb*

## WIT

An original wit is a guy who hears the gag before you do.

Strange! that a man who has wit enough to write a satire, should have folly enough to publish it.

If you want to be witty, work on your character and say what you think on every occasion.
*Stendhal*

A man often runs the risk of throwing away a witticism if he admits that it is his own.
*Jean de la Bruyère*

An ounce of wit is worth a pound of sorrow.

Plagued with an itching leprosy of wit.
*Benjamin Jonson*

Even wit is a burden when it talks too long.
*Latin proverb*

Wit is far more often a shield than a lance.
*Anonymous*

Wit is a sword; it is meant to make people feel the point as well as see it.
*G. K. Chesterton*

Surprise is so essential an ingredient of wit that no wit will bear repetition.
*Sydney Smith*

Wit ought to be a glorious treat, like caviar; never spread it about like marmalade.
*Noel Coward*

When the ale is in, the wit is out.

Wit is the salt of conversation, not the food.
*William Hazlitt*

## WOMEN

By the time a man can read a woman like a book, he needs bifocals.

A beautiful lady is an accident of nature. A beautiful old lady is a work of art.
*Louis Nizer*

A lady's imagination is very rapid; it jumps from admiration to love, from love to matrimony, in a moment.
*Jane Austen*

What passes for woman's intuition is often nothing more than man's transparency.
*George Jean Nathan*

It is better to dwell in a corner of the housetop, than with a brawling woman in a wide house.
*Proverbs 21:9*

When the fine eyes of a woman are veiled with tears it is the man who no longer sees clearly.
*Achille Tournier*

Women are never stronger than when they arm themselves with their weaknesses.
*Madame du Deffand*

Some women are not beautiful—they only look as though they are.

Nothing is more moving than beauty which is unaware of itself, except for ugliness which is.
*Robert Mallet*

## WONDER
Wonder is the basis of worship.
*Thomas Carlyle*

## WOOD
Ye cannot see the wood for the trees.

## WOOING
A man chases a woman until she catches him.
*American proverb*

## WORD
But words once spoke can never be recall'd.
*Wentworth Dillon*

Let thy words be few.
*Ecclesiastes 5:2*

Words are the most powerful drug used by mankind.
*Rudyard Kipling*

A word spoken in due season, how good it is!
*Proverbs 15:23*

The words of his mouth were smoother than butter, but war was in his heart: his words were softer than oil, yet were they drawn swords.
*Psalm 55:21*

Man does not live by words alone, despite the fact that sometimes he has to eat them.
*Adlai Stevenson*

A word fitly spoken is like apples of gold in pictures of silver.
*Proverbs 25:11*

He that hath knowledge spareth his words.
*Proverbs 17:27*

Sharp words make more wounds than surgeons can heal.

Eating words has never given me indigestion.
*Winston Churchill*

"When I use a word," Humpty Dumpty said in rather a scornful tone, "it means just what I choose it to mean—neither more nor less."
"The question is," said Alice, "whether you can make words mean so many different things."
"The question is," said Humpty Dumpty, "which is to be master—that's all."
*Lewis Carroll*

A single word often betrays a great design.
*Jean Baptiste Racine*

Always keep your words soft and sweet—one day you may have to eat them.

## WORK

When it comes to work, there are many who will stop at nothing.

Work is something that when we have it, we wish we didn't, and when we don't have it, we wish we did.

An unfulfilled vocation drains the color from a man's entire existence.
*Honoré de Balzac*

The ugliest of trades have their moments of pleasure. Now, if I was a grave digger, or even a hangman, there are some people I could work for with a great deal of enjoyment.
*D. W. Jerrold*

Elbow grease gives the best polish.

Choose a job you love, and you will never have to work a day in your life.
*Confucius*

God gives the nuts, but he does not crack them.

Every man's work shall be made manifest.
*1 Corinthians 3:13*

The labourer is worthy of his hire.
*Luke 10:7*

As a remedy against all ills—poverty, sickness, and melancholy—only one thing is absolutely necessary: a liking for work.
*Charles Baudelaire*

The one who is unwilling to work shall not eat.
*2 Thessalonians 3:10 (NIV)*

Under the spreading chestnut tree
The village smithy stands;
The smith a mighty man is he
With large and sinewy hands.
And the muscles of his brawny arms
Are strong as iron bands.
He earns whatever he can,
His brow is wet with honest sweat,
And looks the whole world in the face,
For he owes not any man.
*Henry W. Longfellow*

The man who rolls up his shirt sleeves is rarely in danger of losing his shirt.
*Anonymous*

It is working that makes a workman.

The average person puts only 25 percent of his energy and ability into his work. The world takes off its hat to those who put in more than 50 percent of their capacity, and stands on its head for those few and far between souls who devote 100 percent.
*Andrew Carnegie*

All work and no play makes Jack a dull boy—and Jill a
wealthy widow.
*Evan Esar*

There is no substitute for hard work.
*Thomas Edison*

Work is no disgrace; the disgrace is idleness.
*Greek proverb*

When I die, may I be taken in the midst of work.
*Ovid*

Many hands make light work.

Work expands so as to fill the time available for its completion.
*C. Northcote Parkinson*

## WORLD

All the world's a stage, And all the men and women merely
players.
*William Shakespeare*

## WORRY

Worry is the interest paid on trouble before it falls due.

It pays to worry. Ninety percent of the things I worry about
never happen. Worry keeps them away.

He'd give the devil ulcers.
*Anonymous*

It is not work that kills men; it is worry. Worry is rust upon
the blade.
*Henry Ward Beecher*

## WOUND

If you can't heal the wound, don't tear it open.
*Danish proverb*

A wound heals, but the scar remains.

None can speak of a wound with skill, if he hath not a wound
felt.

They that are afraid of wounds must not come near a battle.

## WRINKLE

An old wrinkle never wears out.

Wrinkles should merely indicate where smiles have been.
*Mark Twain*

## WRITER

The whole duty of a writer is to please and satisfy himself, and
the true writer always plays to an audience of one.
*William Strunk*

Talent alone cannot make a writer. There must be a man
behind the book.
*Ralph Waldo Emerson*

Nothing gives an author so much pleasure as to find his works
respectfully quoted by other learned authors.
*Benjamin Franklin*

Advice to young writers who want to get ahead without any
annoying delays: don't write about Man, write about a man.
*E. B. White*

We like that a sentence should read as if its author, had he
held a plough instead of a pen, could have drawn a furrow
deep and straight to the end.
*Henry David Thoreau*

A first edition of his work is a rarity, but a second is rarer still.
*Franklin Pierce Adams*

A writer and nothing else: a man alone in a room with the
English language, trying to get human feelings right.
*John K. Hutchens*

Writers seldom write the things they think. They simply write
the things they think other folks think they think.
*Elbert Hubbard*

You become a good writer just as you become a good joiner:
by planing down your sentences.

# WRITING

Writing is no trouble: you just jot down ideas as they occur to you. The jotting is simplicity itself—it is the occurring which is difficult.
*Stephen Leacock*

In any really good subject, one has only to probe deep enough to come to tears.
*Edith Wharton*

It is a sobering thought that each of us gives his hearers and his readers a chance to look into the inner working of his mind when he speaks or writes.
*J. M. Barker*

Vigorous writing is concise. A sentence should contain no unnecessary words, a paragraph no unnecessary sentences, for the same reason that a drawing should have no unnecessary lines and a machine no unnecessary parts. This requires not that the writer make all his sentences short, or that he avoid all detail and treat his subjects only in outline, but that every word tell.
*William Strunk*

I conceive that the right way to write a story for boys is to write so that it will not only interest boys but strongly interest any man who has ever been a boy. That immensely enlarges the audience.
*Mark Twain*

Better to write for yourself and have no public, than to write for the public and have no self.
*Cyril Connolly*

I write for myself and strangers. The strangers, dear Readers, are an after-thought.
*Gertrude Stein*

I think it's bad to talk about one's present work, for it spoils something at the root of the creative act. It discharges the tension.
*Norman Mailer*

The greatest thing in style is to have a command of metaphor.
*Aristotle*

Make 'em laugh; make 'em cry; make 'em wait.
*Charles Reade*

Once in seven years I burn all my sermons; for it is a shame if I cannot write better sermons now than I did seven years ago.
*John Wesley*

When we see a natural style we are quite amazed and delighted, because we expected to see an author and find a man.
*Blaise Pascal*

Nothing goes by luck in composition. It allows of no tricks. The best you can write will be the best you are. Every sentence is the result of a long probation. The author's character is read from title-page to end. Of this he never corrects the proofs.
*Henry David Thoreau*

## WRONG

It is better to suffer wrong than to do it, and happier to be sometimes cheated than not to trust.
*Samuel Johnson*

We ought never to do wrong when people are looking.
*Mark Twain*

The man who says, "I may be wrong, but—" does not believe there can be any such possibility.
*Kin Hubbard*

YOUTH

# YOUTH

This is a youth-oriented society, and the joke is on them because youth is a disease from which we all recover.
*Anonymous*

It costs a great deal to be reasonable; it costs youth.
*Madame de La Fayette*

Don't laugh at a youth for his affectations; he's only trying on one face after another till he finds his own.
*Logan Pearsall Smith*

It is always self-defeating to pretend to the style of a generation younger than your own; it simply erases your own experience in history.
*Renata Adler*

Let no man despise thy youth.
*1 Timothy 4:12*

Remember now thy Creator in the days of thy youth.
*Ecclesiastes 12:1*

Youth is that period when a young boy knows everything but how to make a living.
*Carey Williams*

During the first period of a man's life the greatest danger is: not to take the risk.
*S. A. Kierkegaard*

One stops being a child when one realizes that telling one's trouble does not make it better.
*Cesare Pavese*

The denunciation of the young is a necessary part of the hygiene of older people, and greatly assists the circulation of the blood.
*Logan Pearsall Smith*

Z

ZEAL

## ZEAL

It is good to be zealously affected always in a good thing.
*Galatians 4:18*

Zeal without knowledge is a runaway horse.

There is no greater sign of a general decay of virtue in a
nation, than a want of zeal in its inhabitants for the good of
their country.
*Joseph Addison*

# About the Author

**BOB PHILLIPS, PHD,** is a licensed marriage and family counselor. He is a cofounder of the Pointman Leadership Institute, which has presented leadership seminars in over seventy countries worldwide. Bob is the executive director emeritus for Hume Lake Christian Camps, one of America's largest youth camping programs. He is also a *New York Times* bestselling author with over 130 titles and over 11 million copies in print. These include *Leadership Success in 10 Minutes a Day, Overcoming Anxiety and Depression,* and *Attitude Is a Choice—So Pick a Good One.* Bob has a BA from Biola University, an MA in counseling from Cal State University in Fresno, and a PhD in counseling from Trinity Seminary. He and his wife, Pam, have two daughters and three grandsons, and live in California.